PROBLEMS

IN

INSURANCE LAW

JAMES R. DEVINE
PROFESSOR OF LAW
UNIVERSITY OF MISSOURI-COLUMBIA SCHOOL OF LAW

NICOLAS P. TERRY
PROFESSOR OF LAW
ST. LOUIS UNIVERSITY SCHOOL OF LAW

AMERICAN CASEBOOK SERIES

WEST PUBLISHING COMPANY
ST. PAUL, MINNESOTA
1989

ISBN 0-314-56417-9

PREFACE

Law students and lawyers do not think of Insurance Law as one of the deeply philosophical areas of legal study. Yet in the latter part of the 20th Century, Insurance, its cost and availability, is an area which shapes virtually all of the substantive and procedural areas of American jurisprudence. At some point in a course in Insurance Law, the principles of Contracts; Torts; Federal, State and Local Government Law; Evidence; Trial Practice; Legislation; Family Law; Antitrust; Property; and Legal Ethics all become a part of the course of study. Indeed, even Jurisprudence is involved in determining the appropriate reparation system for society's members injured as a result of the conduct of another. Because Insurance focuses on that most basic human trait--the ability to err--it is an area of study which of necessity touches on all areas of law.

It is, however, the human element--the ability of people and business to work their way into so many odd situations--that distinguishes insurance from many of these other courses of study. It is to that human element that this book is addressed.

Few lawyers will manage to avoid all insurance problems. Even though the particular insurance legal principle may be simple, complexity is added because of the personal twist this insurer or insured added to teachings of prior law. The result is that no two insurance law problems are ever the same because the people involved in the event which produces the need for insurance are rarely the same.

This book is designed to augment traditional case and treatise readings in Insurance Law and to give students additional fact patterns within which to apply the legal principles taken from those other cases and readings.

Throughout the problems, the authors have tried to be neutral to gender and nationality. Choice of a particular sex in a problem, or use of a particular name is not in any way designed to convey the authors' feelings or beliefs about the habits or traits of the particular sex or nationality which might be represented. Likewise, choice of a name for an Insurance Company or Agency is not designed to disparage any company or agency. Where an actual name is used, it comes directly from a case. Where a fictional name is used, it is indeed fictional, used without any intent to convey emotion or value.

After many of the individual and all of the sections of problems in this book are references to the following student texts and hornbooks:

E. Fischer & P. Swisher, Insurance Law (Mathew Bender, 1986)

R. Henderson, Insurance Law (Michie, 1989)

R. Jerry, Understanding Insurance Law (Matthew Bender, 1987)

R. Keeton & A. Widiss, Insurance Law (West, 1988)

R. Keeton, Basic Insurance Law (West, 1977)

A. Widiss, Insurance (West, 1989)

K. York & J. Whelan, Insurance Law (2d Ed.) (West, 1988)

W. Young & E. Holmes, Insurance (Foundation, 1985)

The book has not been cross-referenced with R. Keeton & A. Widiss, 1988 *Course Supplement on Insurance Law*, (West, 1988) as that book is cross-referenced in the Keeton & Widiss Hornbook.

Preface

Many of the Problems are taken from actual cases, although considerable liberty has been taken with the facts of such cases to produce problems manageable in a law school classroom.

The Problems themselves pose single and multiple issue Questions. Many of the problems are designed to provide an outline structure for an entire class session, in which multiple issues within a particular sub-field are considered. In addition, several of the Problems presume further Instructor attention. When a Problem is designed to point out the provision of a state's insurance code, the Problem directs the student to look for the statutory provision.

No project of this type is possible without the kind and generous assistance of many people. Professor Devine wishes to thank the secretarial staff at the University of Missouri-Columbia, and especially Mary Deardeuff, for help in manuscript preparation, his insurance law students at the University of Missouri and at summer schools at the University of North Carolina and Washington University-St. Louis for input into the factual situations presented here, and Randy Wiemer, UMC law, '83 for keeing the computers running.

Finally, but foremost, Professor Devine thanks Zack, Josh, Noah, and especially Sharon for continuing to be the best insurance that a father and husband could seek.

Professor Terry wishes to thank his insurance law students for their patience, understanding and cheerful incomprehension, and Ellen Edwards and Jonathan Edwards Terry for sharing computer time with him.

July 1, 1989

James R. Devine
Nicolas P. Terry

Summary of Contents

Page

CONTENTS

Page

Chapter 4: Insurance Marketing Problems

CHAPTER 8: AUTOMOBILE INSURANCE

CHAPTER ONE

INSURANCE IN CONTEXT

A. INSURANCE DEFINED

PROBLEM 1

As young, aspiring law students, Abel, Baker and Crouch were concerned about the potential of failing the upcoming bar examination. Accordingly, after completing a law school course in Insurance, they contacted the Underwriters at Lloyds and sought an Insurance Policy against failing the bar examination.

The Students first received this proposal from the Underwriters:

> For a premium payment of $500, the Underwriters will insure the person named herein (insured) against failure on the bar examination in (here fill in name of state). In the event the insured does fail the bar examination, recovery under this policy shall be limited to the lesser of a.) the actual salary lost by insured between the date notice of failure is received by insured and the date the next succeeding bar results are announced OR

b.) $500.

Upon further negotiation, the law students advised Underwriters that they had job offers which required that they pass the bar. Abel was to be employed as a Judicial Clerk for an annual salary of $32,000; Baker had accepted a job as a prosecutor at a salary of $33,000 and Crouch was going into private practice at a large firm for a salary of $55,000. The Underwriters also knew that about 6 months would pass between the time an applicant learned of failure on the bar and the time the next bar results would be announced. Thereafter, the law students received from the underwriters the following proposal:

> In return for premium payments of $40 per month payable during the months the person named herein (the Insured) is actually enrolled in law school, the Underwriters will insure the insured against failure on the bar examination of <u>(here fill in name of state)</u>. In the event the insured does fail the bar examination, recovery under this policy shall be limited to the lesser of a.) the actual salary lost by insured between the date notice of failure is received by insured and the date the next succeeding bar results are announced OR b.) $16,000.

Attached to this proposal was the notation: "If any person insured hereunder is chosen for the Law Review or qualifies for the Dean's List for two (2) consecutive semesters, such person will receive a 15% discount on all further premium payments."

Also attached to the proposal was a set of "CONDITIONS:"

> As an Express Condition of the insurance coverage hereunder, the insured represents and agrees:

1. That the insured will continue enrollment at a law school approved by the American Bar Association; and

2. That prior to taking the bar examination, insured will enroll in, at insured's expense, a bar review course approved by the Underwriters.

Questions

1. Is the first proposal Insurance?
2. Is the second proposal Insurance?
3. What purpose is served by a discount?
4. What is the purpose of the Conditions?

Notes

E. FISCHER & P. SWISHER, Principles of Insurance Law, Introduction at xxi (Matthew Bender, 1986); R. JERRY, Understanding Insurance Law, §10 (Matthew Bender, 1987); R. KEETON & A. WIDISS, Insurance Law, §1.1; 1.3 (West, 1988); R. KEETON, Basic Insurance Law, Excerpts, p. 906, *Jordan v. Group Health Ass'n.*, p. 908; *McCarty v. King County Medical Service Corp.*, p. 921; *McIntosh v. Group Health Ass'n.*, p. 921; *Commissioner of Internal Revenue v. Treganowan*, p. 947 (West, 1977); A. WIDISS, Insurance, §§1.1; 1.2 (West, 1989); K. YORK & J. WHELAN, Insurance Law (Second Edition), notes, pp. 2-3; *Griffin Systems, Inc. v. Washburn*, p. 3; *Truta v. Avis Rent A Car Sys., Inc.*, p. 6 (West, 1988).

B. Insurance Distinguished from Other Transactions

Problem 2

In connection with the sale of its "Tiger" line of new cars, The Bengal Motor Car Company offers to customers an optional "5 year, 50,000 mile owner protection insurance plan." That plan provides coverage as follows:

> Bengal Motor Car Company will repair or replace, at its option, any portion of the insured automobile which proves defective because of faulty parts or workmanship in design, assembly, transport or delivery of such motor vehicle for a period of 5 years from the date hereof or 50,000 odometer miles, whichever occurs first.

The Bengal Motor Car Company stopped doing any business in your state, because of a disagreement with auto emission rules. Regina Smith had purchased a "Tiger" car two years ago prior to the Company stopping business. Regina's "Tiger" now had 25,000 miles on it. When she purchased the car, she also purchased, at additional cost, the "owner protection insurance plan." After unsuccessful negotiation following a defect in the car, Regina's attorney attempted to sue The Bengal Motor Car Company and effect service of process upon the State Commissioner of Insurance, alleging that the "owner protection insurance plan" brought Bengal within the definition of Insurance. Bengal appeared only for the purpose of seeking to quash service of process on this basis. What result?

Problem 3

Davis Roofing Supply Co. agreed to supply roofing materials to Jones Brothers Builders for use in a job to be performed by Jones Brothers for the Ames Elementary School. There was no relationship between Davis Roofing Supply Co. and Jones Brothers, other than the contract to supply. The installation of the roof was exclusively the province of Jones Brothers. In their supply contract, Davis Roofing Supply Co. agreed as follows:

> Davis Roofing Supply Co. agrees to repair damage to the roofing membrane and base flashing resulting from leaks caused by natural deterioration of the roofing membrane or base flashing, blisters, bare spots, fish mouths, ridges, splits not caused by structural failure, buckles and wrinkles, thermal shock, gravel stop breaks, plastic pans, workmanship in applying the membrane and base flashing, and slippage of the Davis Roofing Supply Co. products.

Jones Brothers has an insurance policy with what is referred to as an "escape clause." Under the clause, Jones' Insurance Company has no liability whatsoever if there is other valid insurance for the loss. After a dispute arose because of defective installation of the roof, with the result that both Jones Brothers and Davis Roofing Supply Co. were sued as defendants by the Board of Education of Ames, the Insurance Company filed a declaratory judgment action seeking to be excused from defense because the contract clause by Davis Roofing Supply Co. constitutes insurance. Is this contention correct?

Notes

E. FISCHER & P. SWISHER, Principles of Insurance Law, *Guaranteed Warranty Corp. v. Arizona*, p. 670; notes & questions, pp. 672-73 (Matthew Bender, 1987); R. HENDERSON, Insurance Law Cases & Materials, *GAF Corp. v. County School Bd.*, p. 1; notes, p. 3 (Michie, 1989); R. KEETON & A. WIDISS, Insurance Law, §8.3 (West, 1988); R. KEETON, Basic Insurance Law, Excerpts, p. 906; *Transportation Guarantee Co. v. Jellins*, p. 923; *Feinstein v. Attorney-General*, p. 933; *Continental Auto Club, Inc. v. Navarre*, p. 938; *State ex rel Duffy v. Western Auto Supply Co.*, p. 939; *State ex rel Herbert v. Standard Oil Co.*, p. 941; *State ex rel Attorney General v. Smith Funeral Home Service, Inc.*, p. 942; *Guaranteed Warranty Corp. v. State ex rel Humphrey*, p. 943 (West, 1977); A. WIDISS, Insurance, *Prepaid Dental Services, Inc. v. Day*, p. 929; notes, p. 932 (West, 1989); K. YORK & J. WHELAN, Insurance Law (Second Edition), *Griffin Systems, Inc. v. Washburn*, p. 3; *Truta v. Avis Rent A Car System, Inc.*, p. 6; notes, pp. 10-14; *Wilson v. All Service Ins. Corp.*, p. 14 (West, 1988); W. YOUNG & E. HOLMES, Insurance (Second Edition), *GAF Corp. v. County School Board*, p. 38; notes, p. 40; notes 2-4, p. 43; Doctor-Patient

Plans, p. 52; note, p. 53 (Foundation, 1985).

C. THE "BUSINESS OF INSURANCE"

PROBLEM 4

Provident Insurance Company, a licensed health insurer in your state, has sought to increase its market share of prescription drug insurance business. Your state regulates insurance companies, including Provident, to the full extent permitted by the McCarran-Ferguson Act. In trying to increase its business, Provident has solicited each drug retailer in the state with the following proposal.

> Drug Retailer agrees to sell to each Provident Insured all prescription medications at a cost to the consumer of $2 per prescription. Upon proof of filling the order sent to Provident, Provident will pay to Drug Retailer the actual cost of filling the prescription.

The result of this proposal is that Drug Retailer, in exchange for agreeing to accept a $2 profit on each prescription filled, is virtually assured of collection on all of its prescription sales.

After selling this proposal to druggists, Provident sought and received permission from the state Insurance Commissioner for its plans and then marketed its Prescription Drug Insurance Plan to consumers. For their yearly premium, the consumer paid $2 for each prescription, the remainder of each prescription being paid by Provident pursuant to its agreement with the retailers.

David Katz is a representative of several small drug stores in your area. Katz's drug store is too small to make any profit from a $2 return on each prescription. As a result, Katz turned down Provident's plan. Now, if a Provident consumer buys prescription drugs at Katz's Drugs, the consumer must make a claim direct to Provident which will then pay only 75% of the difference between the actual cost, and $2.

Katz has now filed suit in the United States District Court alleging that Provident and participating Retail Druggists violated section 1 of the Sherman Act by agreeing to fix drug and prescription prices and that their collective activities had caused Provident policy holders not to deal with Katz and the other non-participating stores.

Questions

1. Does the agreement between the drug retailers and Provident impact on the business of insurance?

2. What evidence is necessary to show such an impact?

3. Can Katz sustain a Sherman Act cause of action in the United States District Court?

Problem 5

The Federal Trade Commission would like to charge Local Casualty Co. with deceptive advertising in connection with the offering of life insurance policies in several states. Local Casualty has complied with the Insurance Laws of each of the affected states. Can the FTC successfully allege that the McCarran-Ferguson Act is designed to give the states concurrent jurisdiction with those federal agencies, such as the FTC, which, for the good of the general public, ought to aid in controlling deceptive insurance practices?

Problem 6

Security Life Insurance Co. and Farmers Life Insurance are both licensed life insurers in your state, which has chosen to regulate the business of insurance, within the meaning of the McCarran-Ferguson Act. Security Life and Farmers Life, which are both stock companies, propose to merge and have approval both from the Commissioner of Insurance of your state and from the shareholders of the two companies. Can the Securities and Exchange Commission, consistent with the provisions of the McCarran-Ferguson Act, file suit to stop the merger, alleging violations of the federal securities law?

Problem 7

Insured purchased his most recent automobile insurance policy on credit from Statewide Auto Insurers, a licensed Insurance Company in your state. The policy was financed and paid for over the period of insurance. Insured has now filed suit against Statewide claiming that the insurer failed to clearly, conspicuously, and meaningfully disclose the amount of the finance charge, the total number of payments, the deferred payment price and the annual percentage rate, all in violation of the Federal Truth in Lending Act. Statewide has filed a motion to dismiss. What result? Is there any way that Insured can seek to amend his pleading?

Notes

E. FISCHER & P. SWISHER, Principles of Insurance Law, *Feinstein v. Nettleship Co. of Los Angeles*, p. 673; notes & questions, pp. 678-79 (Matthew Bender, 1987); R. JERRY, Understanding Insurance Law, §21 (Matthew Bender, 1987); R. KEETON & A. WIDISS, Insurance Law, §§8.1(a) & (b) (West, 1988); R. KEETON, Basic Insurance Law, *United States v. South-Eastern Underwriters Ass'n.*, p. 888; McCarran-Ferguson Act, p. 903; Excerpts, p. 904; *Federal Trade Commission v. National Casualty Co.*, p. 905; *Securities & Exchange Comm. v. Variable Annuity Life Ins. Co.*, p. 956; *Department of Insurance v. Motors Ins. Corp.*, p. 968 (West, 1977); A. WIDISS, Insurance, *United States v. South-Eastern Underwriters Ass'n.*, p. 891; note, p. 902; McCarran-Ferguson Act, p. 903; *Union Labor Life Ins. Co. v. Pireno*, p. 904; *Feinstein v. Nettleship Co. of Los Angeles*, p. 912 (West, 1989); K. YORK & J. WHELAN, Insurance Law (Second Edition), notes, pp. 27-28; *Spirt v. Teachers Insurance & Annuity Assoc.*, p. 28; notes, pp. 34-37; questions, pp. 37-38 (West, 1988); W. YOUNG & E. HOLMES, Insurance (Second Edition), The McCarran-Ferguson Act, p. 25; *Union Labor Life Ins. Co. v. Pireno*, p. 27 (Foundation, 1985).

D. Purposes and Types of Insurance

Problem 8

When Sam Davis told his lifelong friend Ed Rousch that Davis' farm tractor was broken and could not be fixed for several months and that, as a result, Davis would likely miss spring planting, Rousch wanted to help. Rousch knew that his farming days were about to end because of his impending bankruptcy, and therefore, he signed over his own recently-purchased tractor to Davis. In doing so, Rousch told Davis that Davis would likely lose the tractor in a couple of months to the trustee in bankruptcy, but that Davis should keep the tractor and use it as much as he could. Davis immediately took the tractor home and began calling it "his." Davis decided that, since he was going to use the tractor, he ought to insure it.

Questions

1. For which of the following might Davis want to buy insurance?

a. The risk that in operating the tractor, the tractor will injure Davis, cause Davis to be hospitalized and incur medical bills?

b. The risk that in operating the tractor, the tractor will injure Davis, cause Davis to be hospitalized and 1.) be required to hire someone to do the planting; and 2.) lose time (and salary) from his regular job as a Printer's Assistant?

c. The risk that a windstorm will damage the tractor?

d. The risk that in operating the tractor, Davis will do something wrong and cause the tractor to be damaged?

e. The risk that in operating the tractor, Davis will cause personal injury to some third party?

2. What type of insurance should Davis buy?

3. Should Davis be prevented from buying insurance for any of these risks? Why?

Notes

R. HENDERSON, Insurance Law Cases & Materials, Types of Insurers and Insurance, p. 12 (Michie, 1989); R. JERRY, Understanding Insurance Law, §§13, 13A, 13B, 13D (Matthew Bender, 1987); R. KEETON & A. WIDISS, Insurance Law, §§1.4, 1.5, 3.1(a),(b) (West, 1988); R. KEETON, Basic Insurance Law, Excerpts, pp. 78-81; Introduction to Indemnity, pp. 121-24 (West, 1977); A. WIDISS, Insurance, §1.5 (West, 1989); K. YORK & J. WHELAN, Insurance Law (Second Edition), Classification of Insurance, pp. 16-20; Pinzur, Insurable Interest: A Search for Consistency, pp. 192-98 (West, 1988).

Chapter Two

State Regulation of Insurance

A. Generally

Problem 9

Mona Roberts is President and sole shareholder of a small insurance company, No Frills Insurance Company, which has been properly incorporated in your state. Mona recently saw a television advertisement in which a former television star, and unfortunately now deceased cancer patient, talked about the benefits of "Cancer Insurance" sponsored by another insurance company. Because cancer insurance is so highly profitable, trading, as it does, on individual fear of the dreaded disease, Mona Roberts is anxious to have her company enter this market. The cancer insurance envisioned by Mona would be a new offering by No Frills and is a type of health insurance known as "Specified Disease Insurance." It can cover as few as one specific disease and is often offered as a rider to existing health insurance coverage. The No Frills policy would cover only "necessary definitive medical treatment" for cancer, and only after that cancer has been positively diagnosed by "a legally licensed doctor of medicine certified by the American Board of Pathology, upon the basis of a microscopic examination of fixed tissue, or preparations from the hemic system (either during life or post mortem)." In addition, the diagnosis must be based "solely on the criteria of malignancy as accepted by the American Board of Pathology."

Mona recalls that in another state, a different insurance company tried to sell Specified Disease Insurance for cancer but was apparently prevented from doing so, unless it was willing to specify at least 12 separate diseases covered by the policy.

Mona and her associates have prepared a model Cancer Insurance Specified Disease Rider and are prepared to offer it on the market.

Questions

Before answering the following questions, you should locate the Insurance Statutes of your State:

1. Before selling Cancer Insurance, must No Frills make any filings with any State agency? Which one? Does it matter if the offering is for a new policy or for a Rider on existing insurance?

2. If any filings are made, what rights does the State have to prevent this offering? How are those rights exercised?

3. How would the State adopt a regulation like that mentioned in the

Problem requiring a specific number of diseases to be covered?

4. What rights does No Frills have to challenge any state determination?

5. As noted by Roberts, cancer insurance is profitable because it plays upon individual fears of cancer. What restrictions exist as to the ability of No Frills to advertise this new policy?

6. How and who should determine the rates charged for this insurance?

Problem 10

Last year, when he renewed his homeowners' insurance policy with The American Interinsurance Co., George South saw, but paid no attention to a note describing an amendment to his policy. Several months later, George's 18 year old son, Wylie, started a fire in the home because he fell asleep while smoking in bed. The fire caused approximately $10,000 damage. American Interinsurance Co. has indicated that they will not pay on this claim because of the new exclusion which had been included in the fire portion of the homeowners policy. That new policy provision excluded from coverage "a fire caused by any member of the household of the named insured." When George phoned his insurance agent, Aaron Towns, to inquire about this exclusion, he was told that American Interinsurance had decided to add this clause because of the increased instances of smoking in bed by family members of insureds. Aaron also told George that the Souths had received a 5% premium reduction over prior year premiums. George has been advised by his attorney that state administrative regulation has mandated that the New York Standard Fire Policy be used throughout the state.

Questions

1. What is the best argument for coverage under the state administrative regulation?

2. Assume that American Interinsurance Co. is not a licensed insurer in George's state. Upon further inquiry, George cannot find an address for Aaron Agent, with whom George always dealt by phone. If George decides that he needs to sue American Interinsurance Co., can that suit be filed in George's state. How can service of process be obtained?

Notes

E. FISCHER & P. SWISHER, Principles of Insurance Law, *Fairmount Ins. Co. v. Commonwealth Ins. Dept.*, p. 679; notes & questions, pp. 681-82; *Minnehoma Ins Co. v. Oklahoma State Board for Prop. & Cas. Rates*, p. 683; notes & questions, p. 686; *Commonwealth Ins. Dept. v. Safeguard Mut. Ins. Co.*, p. 687; *State ex rel. American Indemnity Co. v. Brown*, p. 693; notes & questions, p. 695; *State, Dept. of Ins. v. Insurance Services Office*, p. 697; notes & questions, pp. 701-702 (Matthew Bender, 1987); R. JERRY, Understanding Insurance Law, §§22(a), (e); 23(a) (Matthew Bender, 1987); R. KEETON & A. WIDISS, Insurance Law, §§8.2; 8.3(a); 8.4 (West, 1988); R. KEETON, Basic Insurance Law, *Montgomery v. Daniels* p. 365; Excerpts, pp. 1022-1029; *Federal Crop Ins. Corp. v. Merril*, p. 1030; *Allied American Mutual Fire Ins. Co. v. Commissioner of Motor Vehicles*, p. 1035; *Employers' Liability Assurance Corp. v. Frost*, p. 1039; *California State Automobile Ass'n Inter-Insurance Bureau v. Maloney*, p. 1040; *Factory Mutual Liability Ins. Co. v. Justices of the Superior Court*, p. 1042; *Birdwell v. Tri-State Ins. Co.*, p. 1042 (West, 1977); A. WIDISS, Insurance, *Paulson v. Western Life Ins. Co.*, p. 920; note, p.932; *Massachusetts Automobile Rating & Accident Prevention Bureau v. Commissioner of Ins.*, p. 935; *State of Florida, Department of Ins. v. Insurance Services Office*, p. 945; *Arizona Governing Comm. v. Norris*, p. 959; note, p. 978; Techniques of Governmental Sponsorship, p. 980; Areas of Governmental Sponsorship, p. 981; Collateral Effects of Governmental Sponsorship, p. 982; The Problem of Uninsured Losses, p. 983; The Problem of Unwanted Insureds, p. 984; *Prudential Property and Cas. Ins. Co. v. Insurance Comm. of the South Carolina Department of Ins.*, p. 985 (West, 1989); K. YORK & J. WHELAN, Insurance Law (Second Edition), Notes, pp. 12-14; *Wilson v. All Service Ins. Corp.*, p. 14; *Metz v. Universal Underwriters Ins. Co.*, p. 21; *Pin Pin H. Su v. Kemper Insurance Companies/American Motorists Ins. Co.*, p. 23 (West, 1988); W. YOUNG

& F. HOLMES, Insurance (Second Edition), *Prudential Property and Cas. Ins. Co. v. Insurance Comm. of the South Carolina Department of Ins.*, p. 49 (Foundation, 1985).

B. Cancellation

Problem 11

Gonzales is an amateur racing driver. In February, he applied to Safedriver Insurance for automobile liability coverage. He falsely answered Safedriver's inquiry as to the applicant's participation in motor-sports. In April, Safedriver's local agent discovered the nature of Gonzales' hobby and referred the matter to the company's "central claim committee" which determined that the false answer constituted a material misrepresentation and warranted rescission. On May 15, Safedriver wrote to Gonzales cancelling the policy forthwith and refunding an amount representing the premium paid for the cancelled portion of the policy. This check was never cashed and Gonzales later testified that he did not recall receiving this letter of cancellation. A week later a copy of Safedriver's letter was received by the state drivers' license bureau.

On May 18, Gonzales was involved in an automobile accident in which Boone suffered severe personal injuries. Boone's representatives indicated that they would hold Gonzales responsible. Gonzales tendered the matter to Safedriver for defense. Subsequently, Safedriver's local claims adjuster again wrote to Gonzales denying coverage and indicating that the policy had previously been cancelled.

After the highway department was notified of Gonzales' accident, the department revoked Gonzales' driving permit and filed criminal charges for his alleged breach of the state's financial responsibility law.

Gonzales has filed an action against Safedriver. How should the court rule on the following issues?

Questions

1. Gonzales argues that his un-rebutted testimony that he did not receive the first letter of cancellation entitled him to partial summary judgement on that issue.

2. Safedriver argues that the clear evidence of their intent to cancel entitled them to a ruling that the policy had been cancelled on May 15, as a matter of law.

3. Gonzales argues that, as a matter of public policy, an insurer's right to rescind a liability policy should be eliminated upon the occurrence of an otherwise covered event.

4. Assume that state statute in Gonzales' state contains either of the following two provisions. Is your answer to any of the foregoing questions different under either statute? (These provisions are taken from Maine and Minnesota respectively):

> A. Cancellation may be initiated by either the insurer or the policyholder by providing 30-days written notice to the other for reasons other than non-payment of premium. Any return premium shall be on a pro-rata basis.
>
> If the insurer initiates cancellation for non-payment of premium,

a grace period of not less than 10 days shall be provided.

B. No insurer may cancel a policy of commercial liability insurance during the term of the policy, except for one or more of the following reasons:

> A. nonpayment of premium;
>
> B. misrepresentation or fraud made by or with the knowledge of the insured in obtaining the policy or in pursuing a claim under the policy;
>
> C. actions by the insured that have substantially increased or substantially changed the risk insured;
>
> D. refusal of the insured to eliminate known conditions that increase the potential for loss after notification by the insurer that the condition must be removed;
>
> E. substantial change in the risk assumed, except to the extent that the insurer should reasonably have foreseen the change or contemplated the risk in writing the contract;
>
> F. loss of reinsurance by the insurer which provided coverage to the insurer for a significant amount of the underlying risk insured. . .
>
> G. a determination by the commissioner that the continuation of the policy could place the insurer in violation of the insurance laws of this state; or

H. nonpayment of dues to an association or organization, other than an insurance association or organization, where payment of dues is a prerequisite to obtaining or continuing such insurance.

5. Assume that Safedriver had effectively cancelled Gonzales' liability policy, but for non-payment of the premium. That letter was received by Gonzales on February 10 and indicated that the policy was cancelled immediately, but provided for a grace period of 5 days within which Gonzales could reinstate the policy. State statute, however, required that there be a 10 day grace period. Gonzales died on February 11. On February 22, an omnibus insured under the Gonzales policy was involved in an accident and tendered the defense of the action to Safedriver. What are Safedriver and the Omnibus Insured's best arguments?

Notes

E. FISCHER & P. SWISHER, Principles of Insurance Law, §1.09 (Matthew Bender, 1987); R. JERRY, Understanding Insurance Law, §62A[c] (Matthew Bender, 1987); R. KEETON & A. WIDISS, Insurance Law, §5.11 (West, 1988); R. KEETON, Basic Insurance Law, *Merchants & Farmers Mut. Cas. Co. v. St. Paul-Mercury Indemnity Coy*, p. 575; *Donarski v. Lardy*, p. 577 (West, 1977); A. WIDISS, Insurance, *Rauch v. American Family Ins. Co.*, p. 530 (West, 1989).

CHAPTER THREE

JUDICIAL INTERPRETATION OF THE INSURANCE CONTRACT

A. GENERAL RULES

PROBLEM 12

Continental Graphic sells, rents, and services commercial printing equipment. To protect its printing press investment, Continental purchased an insurance policy from Allied Property and Casualty Co. The Policy covered "Loss to any Printing Press which occurs on premises owned by or rented to the insured." Last year, while installing a Continental Graphics Press on the premises of another business, Continental employees damaged gears in the press. The other business had not yet accepted delivery of the press, which it was to rent, and therefore had no coverage for the damage under its insurance policy. Continental seeks coverage for the printing press damage from Allied.

Questions

1. Assume that Allied declines coverage because the printing press was not "on premises owned by or rented to the insured." Who will win? How will the Court interpret the language of the contract?

2. Assume that Continental claims that, after the loss, one of its officers called one of Allied's claims adjusters and was told that the property would be covered, even if it was not on Continental premises. How does this change your answer?

3. Assume that the Vice President of Continental, who negotiated the Insurance Contract, will testify that he thought, even after reading the contract that the loss would be covered. Does this create an ambiguity?

4. Assume, instead, that the Insurance Policy provided:

> This policy does not apply to that part of any property not on the premises owned by the insured or under the exclusive control of the insured.

Does this cause your answers to change? Why or why not?

Problem 13

Bob's Tavern, a local bar, is covered by an insurance policy from the

Federal Allied Insurance Co. The policy excludes from coverage:

> Any liability imposed upon the insured as an owner or lessor of any premises engaged in the business of manufacturing, selling or distributing alcoholic beverages, by reason of any statute or ordinance pertaining to the sale, gift, distribution or use of any alcoholic beverage.

Allen McTavett had been a patron at Bob's, got drunk, left the bar, and smashed his car into pedestrian Mary Meyers, causing her extensive injuries. Mary has now sued McTavett (who has no insurance) and Bob's Tavern, the latter for common law negligence in the sale of alcohol to McTavett. When Bob's Tavern turned this suit over to Federal Allied, the insurer refused to defend the suit claiming that any damages flowing from the suit were excluded. Is Federal Allied correct? How should the policy be interpreted?

Notes

E. FISCHER & P. SWISHER, Principles of Insurance Law, Three Theories of Insurance Contract Interpretation, p. 2; notes 5-6, p. 7 (Matthew Bender, 1987); R. HENDERSON, Insurance Law Cases & Materials, Introduction, p. 771; Construing Ambiguities, p. 771 (Michie, 1989); R. JERRY, Understanding Insurance Law, §25A (Matthew Bender, 1987); R. KEETON & A. WIDISS, Insurance Law, §§6.1-6.3 (West, 1988); R. KEETON, Basic Insurance Law, *C & J Fertilizer, Inc. v. Allied Mut. Ins. Co.*, p. 599 (West, 1977); A. WIDISS, Insurance, Unconscionable Advantages, p. 598; *C & J Fertilizer, Inc. v. Allied Mut. Ins. Co.*, p. 599; Good Faith and Fair Dealing, p. 610 (West, 1989); K. YORK & J. WHELAN, Insurance Law (Second Edition), Notes, pp. 39-40; Insurance Law Interpretation, pp. 40-45; *Ponder v. Blue Cross of Southern California*, p. 45; notes, pp. 52-54; *Foremost Insurance Co. v. Putzier*, p. 54; notes, pp. 63-65 (West, 1988); W. YOUNG & F. HOLMES, Insurance (Second Edition), Traditional Contract Analysis, p. 55; *Standard Venetian Blind Co. v. American Empire Ins.*, p. 57 (Foundation, 1985).

B. Dealing with Ambiguity

Problem 14

Protesting at a rally called by citizens opposed to United States intervention in any third-world country, the Reverend Michael Dennis, among others, attempted to block entrance to a local federal office building. Because federal workers were thus prevented from entering the building, the actions were deemed to violate a federal law against blocking ingress and egress to a building, and federal marshals were called. Jon Becker, one of the Marshals, told Rev. Dennis, who was then directly blocking the front door, "I'm sorry, Reverend, you will have to move." At the same time, Becker attempted to grasp Rev. Dennis' elbow to escort him away. Rev. Dennis let his body go limp, fell to the floor, and said: "I'm sorry, Officer, but I can't make this easy for you. The Church is vigorously opposed to U.S. intervention in these countries and I must support that position. You will have to carry me out." When Officer Becker attempted to lift Rev. Dennis, Becker suffered a herniated disk in his back. Dennis and his wife have now sued Rev. Dennis for damages as a result of that herniated disk. The Church at which Dennis is a pastor has a liability insurance policy with Dakota Mutual Casualty Co. for all of the ministers. It was issued to the Church itself and covers Rev. Dennis, as well as the other ministers, "while acting within the scope of their respective duties." Dakota Mutual Casualty has refused to defend the claim by the Beckers alleging that the conduct giving rise to the lawsuit was outside the scope of Rev. Dennis' duties. Rev. Dennis has filed a declaratory judgment against Dakota Mutual to determine if coverage exists.

Questions

1. Will the Court or a Jury resolve whether Rev. Dennis was acting within the scope of his employment?

2. Which of the following is admissible evidence in interpreting the phrase:

A. A dictionary definition of the phrase?
B. Testimony of a Superior Minister as to the Church's view of the obligations of a minister?
C. General principles of principal and agent?
D. Church writings on U.S. intervention?

3. Assume that Rev. Dennis argues that he read the provision and thought that it meant that he would be covered whenever his actions were designed to accomplish the overall objectives of the Church. As a result, Rev. Dennis claims that the jury should be allowed to determine that the policy was ambiguous. What result?

Problem 15

As part of the insurance coverage on their home, Ralph and Doris Stafford had coverage for damage to the home. A portion of that policy provided:

> This policy does not cover loss caused by inherent vice, wear and tear, deterioration; rust, rot, mold or other fungi; dampness of

> atmosphere, extreme of temperature; contamination; vermin, termites, moths or other insects.

A squirrel climbed into the Stafford home through the chimney and caused damage. The insurer refuses to pay for that damage claiming that squirrels are "vermin." Will the Staffords recover their loss?

PROBLEM 16

The Accounting firm of Roberts and Madden purchased an insurance policy from Federal Insurance Co. covering losses from the fraudulent acts of Roberts and Madden agents. In an effort to get the firm to fire employees found to be dishonest, the policy provided that coverage of any employee would terminate "as soon as the Insured shall learn of any dishonest or fraudulent act or acts on the part of any such Employee." After this policy was effective, the firm hired Ronald Stewart as an accountant. At the time Stewart was hired, the officers at Roberts and Madden knew that Stewart had been investigated and disciplined by the State Accountancy Board for dishonest client dealings while employed by another firm. Because Stewart's recent record was clear, and no further trouble had developed, he was hired. Several years later, Roberts and Madden learned that Stewart was committing fraudulent acts when the firm was sued by a series of clients. Stewart was immediately discharged. When Roberts and Madden turned the suits over to Federal for defense, the company refused, indicating that the firm should not have hired Stewart because of their knowledge of his prior dishonesty.

Because that dishonesty was known, and because Stewart was not immediately terminated, there could be no coverage under the policy. How should Roberts and Madden argue in response?

Notes

E. FISCHER & P. SWISHER, Principles of Insurance Law, Three Theories of Insurance Contract Interpretation, p. 2 (Matthew Bender, 1987); R. HENDERSON, Insurance Law Cases & Materials, Construing Ambiguities, p. 771 (Michie, 1989); R. KEETON & A. WIDISS, Insurance Law, §6.2(a) (West, 1988); R. KEETON, Basic Insurance Law, *C.& J. Fertilizer v. Allied Mut. Ins. Co.*, p. 599 (West, 1977); A. WIDISS, Insurance, *C.& J. Fertilizer, Inc. v. Allied Mut. Ins. Co.*, p. 599; *Rusthoven v. Commercial Standard Ins. Co.*, p. 638 (West, 1989); K. YORK & J. WHELAN, Insurance Law (Second Edition), *Foremost Insurance Co. v. Putzier*, p. 58; notes, pp. 63-65 (West, 1988); W. YOUNG & F. HOLMES, Insurance (Second Edition), *Standard Venetian Blind Co. v. American Empire Ins.*, p. 57; notes, pp. 65-67 (Foundation, 1985).

C. Reasonable Expectations

Problem 17

In the *Continental Graphic v. Allied Property and Casualty Insurance Co.* matter, Problem 12, *supra*, assume that representatives of Continental Graphic told the representatives of Allied that Continental rarely, if ever, kept Printing Presses on Continental premises; indeed that Continental only rented a small office. Continental's sole business was in purchasing such equipment, having it delivered to another's business, then setting up the new equipment and making it operational. The Continental Graphic representative explained all of this to the Allied insurance representative and was told that Allied would attempt to devise a policy to cover these contingencies. Several days later, the Allied representative called the Continental Graphic representative and advised that such a policy had been devised. Thereafter, Continental paid the premium and received the standard Allied policy with the language contained in PROBLEM 12.

Questions

1. Is the language of the policy itself ambiguous?

2. Is Continental Graphics in a better legal position to demand coverage for its loss as a result of these additional facts? Why or why not?

3. Is Continental Graphics in a better or worse position if the representative admits that she read the policy when it was received?

PROBLEM 18

As part of a packet of school-related material which Mr. and Mrs. Richards received at the Parent-Teacher Association meeting the first night of high school for their son Carl, there was a brochure for "Statewide Student Travel and Indemnity Insurance." At the PTA meeting, the high school principal mentioned this insurance indicating that the school board had received the packets from Statewide Indemnity Co. which had requested that it be given out to the students and parents. Mr. and Mrs. Richards looked at the brochure and noticed that the offered insurance was for hospital and other medical care suffered by a student as a result of an accident, which, the brochure indicated would not include accidents resulting from "participation in any interscholastic athletic competition." In addition, the brochure indicated the insurance would pay a death benefit of $10,000 if the student died as a result of a travel accident. Because the premium was not too high, Mr. and Mrs. Richards, along with several other families seated near them, purchased the insurance and several weeks later received a policy in the mail from Statewide. The letter accompanying the policy indicated "**PLEASE READ THE ENCLOSED INSURANCE POLICY CAREFULLY.**" Mr. Richards reviewed the policy, and under Exclusions, noticed that accidents "resulting from participation in any interscholastic athletic competition" was not covered. In addition, under the Travel Benefit, Mr. Richards noticed, but did not think about, the provision indicating that a $10,000 death benefit would be paid if death resulted from "any accident while the insured is engaged in travel other than travel as a full time student."

Carl Richards, shortly after entering high school, became something of a star football player. About one month after his parents received the Statewide insurance policy, the school bus taking Carl and his teammates to a football game at another high school overturned. Carl, severely injured, was hospitalized for 10 days, following which he succumbed to his injuries and died.

Questions

1. Statewide has refused to pay the death benefit to Carl's parents claiming that Carl died as a result of an accident while traveling as a full time student and, as a result, was not covered at the time.

   a. Is the policy itself ambiguous on coverage for travel?

b. What facts weigh in favor of granting relief to Mr. and Mrs. Richards?

c. Will the fact that Mr. Richards read the particular policy provision automatically preclude recovery? Why or why not?

2. Assume that Statewide agrees to pay the death benefit, but refuses to pay the medical bills incurred by Carl while in the hospital because they were suffered as a result of "participation in any interscholastic athletic competition." Discuss.

Problem 19

Carton's of Newbridge, a new exclusive jeweler, purchased burglary insurance from Franklin Indemnity Co. That insurance was purchased from Franklin by Clarence Dolby, an agent of Franklin Indemnity and the person who had sold insurance to Ray Carton in several prior business ventures. Several months after the policy became effective, Carton was shocked to see the interior of his store in shambles one morning when he entered. He checked his safe, found it had been opened, and a considerable amount of valuable jewelry removed. When the police arrived, they found that an air conditioning grate had been removed. In addition, police found mud from small shoes on the floor. The police assume that a small child made entry from the outside through the air conditioning grate (the only area of outside access to the air conditioning system was located near an area recently soaked by rain), opened the door to the outside and allowed an adult to enter. Access to the air ducts can be accomplished through a metal door, which is not locked as it is quite small. Thus, the key for the police was the mud from small shoes directly beneath where the air duct had apparently been removed and then successfully replaced. Although police found several partial fingerprints, they have not been able to identify the robbers, although there is no evidence to suspect that the robbery was conducted by Carton, or anyone associated with him. Franklin Indemnity has refused to pay the $250,000 loss claimed by Carton, based upon the burglary provision of the policy. While the policy provides coverage for "loss due to burglary," the definitions section of the policy define burglary as follows:

> Burglary is hereby defined as the felonious abstraction of insured property (1) from within the premises by a person making felonious entry therein by actual force and violence, of which force and violence there are visible marks made by tools, explosives, electricity or chemicals upon, or physical damage to, the exterior of the premises at the place of such entry, or (2) from felonious exit therefrom by actual force and violence as evidenced by visible marks made by tools, explosives, electricity or chemicals upon, or physical damage to, the interior of the premises at the place of such exit.

Now that he has read this provision, Carton agrees that, on the facts, it would not appear that his loss was covered.

Questions

1. Is there anything that can be done to help Carton?

2. How does your analysis change if the Policy itself is called an "All Risk Insurance Policy," or "Comprehensive Crime Coverage?"

PROBLEM 20

Ellen Davis had her car stolen from the driveway of her home. At the time, she had left the keys in the ignition. Unfortunately, the thief crashed the car into another car causing extensive property damage. The thief has disappeared and the owner of the damaged car has sued Ellen for the damage. Ellen's automobile insurance policy with All Risk Insurance Co. defines "insured" for the purpose of coverage under the policy as "the named insured or any person operating the insured vehicle with the permission of the named insured." In a declaratory judgment action filed by Ellen, a trial court has ruled that All Risk must pay the damage claim because, by leaving the key in the ignition, Ellen gave permission. The Trial Court, in a short opinion, wrote:

> This case falls clearly within the Doctrine of Reasonable Expectations, as originally espoused by Professor (now Judge) Keeton. That doctrine holds that where ambiguities exist in an insurance policy, such ambiguities must be resolved in accord with the reasonable expectations of the policy holder.
>
> In this case, I find that ambiguity exists in the definition of the word "insured." Plaintiff Davis has testified that she would have thought herself covered. Thus, under the doctrine of reasonable expectations, there must be coverage.

How should Counsel for All Risk argue the case, now on appeal?

Notes

E. FISCHER & P. SWISHER, Principles of Insurance Law, Introduction, p. 50; *Karl v. New York Life Ins. Co.*, p. 51; notes & questions, pp. 53-55; Effect of Reformation, p. 55; *Western Casualty & Surety Co. v. Sliter*, p. 56; notes & questions, p. 58; Effect of Lack of Disclosure, p. 58; *Selected Risks Ins. Co.*

v. Bruno, p. 59 (Matthew Bender, 1986); R. HENDERSON, Insurance Law, *Collister v. Nationwide Life Ins. Co.*, p. 790; notes, p. 803; *C. & J. Fertilizer, Inc. v. Allied Mutual Ins. Co.*, p. 803; notes, pp. 817-18 (Michie, 1989); R. JERRY, Understanding Insurance Law, §25D (Matthew Bender, 1987); R. KEETON & A. WIDISS, Insurance Law, §6.3 (West, 1988); R. KEETON, Basic Insurance Law, *Steven v. Fidelity & Cas. Co.*, p. 90; *Old American Ins. Co.*, p. 107; *C & J Fertilizer, Inc. v. Allied Mut. Ins. Co.*, p. 599; *Herzog v. National Am. Ins. Co.*, p. 619 (West, 1977); A. WIDISS, Insurance, *Kronfeld v. Fidelity & Cas. Co. of N.Y.*, p. 97; Emergence of Reasonable Expectations, p. 611; *C. & J. Fertilizer, Inc. v. Allied Mut. Ins. Co.*, p. 614; *Markline Co., Inc. v. The Travelers Ins. Co.*, p. 618; *Standard Venetian Blind Co. v. American Empire Ins.*, p. 644; Statutory & Administrative Actions, p. 655; *Gray v. Zurich Ins. Co.*, p. 807 (West, 1989); K. York & J. Whelan, Insurance Law (Second Edition), Insurance Law Interpretation, pp. 40-45; *Ponder v. Blue Cross of Southern California*, p. 45; notes, pp. 52-54 (West, 1988); W. YOUNG & E. HOLMES, Insurance, *Standard Venetian Blind Co. v. American Empire Ins.*, p. 57; *Thompson v. Occidental Life Ins. Co. of California*, p. 72; *Corgatelli v. Globe Life & Acc. Ins. Co.*, p. 75; notes, p. 77; *Estrin Construction Co. v. Aetna Cas. & Surety Co.*, p. 77; notes, pp. 81-83; *C. & J. Fertilizer Inc. v. Allied Mut. Ins. Co.*, p. 83; *Farm Bureau Mut. Ins. Co. v. Sandbulte*, p. 87; notes, pp. 89-91 (Foundation, 1985).

Chapter Four

Insurance Marketing Problems

A. Oral Contracts of Insurance

Problem 21

Eight years ago, Donald Heil purchased a lot with a mobile home on it. He insured both with the Farmer's Insurance Company under what was called a "Five Year Policy," which called for yearly premiums to be paid over the next five year period. Heil paid each such premium. Three years ago, Heil did not receive a premium notice. He does not recall specifically thinking about it, although now tracking his premium payments, he knows that he did not get a premium notice. Last month, Heil met Carter, who had been the agent who sold Heil the Farmer's Insurance policy. Carter asked Heil who was writing Heil's trailer insurance. When Heil, surprised, answered "Farmers," Carter responded: "No they aren't. The company only writes policies for one five year period. After that, you must fill out a new application so the Company can reexamine the risk. As there was no new application, your policy was not renewed three years ago." It was at that point that Heil first realized that he had no insurance. Heil told Carter that Heil wanted immediate insurance on the property, but that the amount of coverage should be raised. Carter quoted Heil a figure of "approximately $450" per year. Three days later, the trailer burned. When Heil reported the loss to Farmer's, coverage was denied.

Questions

1. Heil has sued Farmer's Insurance Company, alleging that an oral contract of insurance was formed when Heil and Carter discussed coverage. While Farmer's admits that Carter was Farmer's agent, and would have authority to bind Farmer's to a contract of insurance, the company denies that an oral contract of insurance would be valid. Discuss.

2. Farmer's also argues that, since it only writes insurance contracts for five year periods, any oral contract to renew would also be for five years and would violate the Statute of Frauds. Discuss.

Notes

E. FISCHER & P. SWISHER, Principles of Insurance Law, Introduction, p. 8; *Gulf Ins. Co. v. Grisham*, p. 9; Notes & Questions, p. 12 (Matthew Bender, 1986); R. HENDERSON, Insurance Law, Notes, p. 835 (Michie, 1989); R. JERRY, Understanding Insurance Law, §§32[d], 33[b] (Matthew Bender, 1987); R. KEETON & A. WIDISS, Insurance Law, §2.2 (West, 1988); R. KEETON, Basic Insurance Law, *Milwaukee Bedding Co. v. Graebner*, p. 62; *Julien v. Spring Lake Park Agency, Inc.*, p. 67; *Nelson v. Glens Falls Ins. Co.*, p. 70; *Boston Camping Distributor Co. v. Lumbermens Mut. Cas. Co.*, p. 72 (West, 1977); A. WIDISS, Insurance, *Gulf Ins. Co. v. Grisham*, p. 34; *Nu-Air Manufacturing Co. v. Frank B. Hall & Co.*, p. 38 (West, 1989); K. YORK & J. WHELAN, Insurance Law (Second Edition), *Maryland Casualty Co. v. J.M. Foster*, p. 79 (West, 1988).

B. Marketing Life and Health Insurance

Problem 22

Tim Helm, an agent for the Parapluie Indemnity Co., persuaded Ellis Godiva to apply for life insurance naming the plaintiff, Frankie Godiva, as beneficiary. Godiva filled out an application form for Parapluie which included a number of medical history questions; paid two months premiums in advance and, in return, Helm issued to Godiva a receipt containing the following:

> Conditions and Effective Date
>
> The Insurance which you, Ellis Godiva, have applied for will be effective from the application date, February 29, if and only if all of these conditions have been complied with:
>
> 1. The full premium accompanies this application.
> 2. You have completed any required medical examination form, and
> 3. We, Parapluie Indemnity Co., have determined by our guidelines that you, Ellis Godiva, and your beneficiaries are qualified for the type and amount of insurance applied for.

On April 12, a Parapluie underwriter notified agent Helm that Ellis Godiva would be required to submit to a medical examination. Helm wrote to Godiva informing him of this development on April 19. However, Ellis Godiva had died on April 13. Helm notified Parapluie of this development, after which Parapluie returned the premiums paid with an explanatory letter stating that it was withdrawing Godiva's application "because of his failure to have a medical examination."

Frankie Godiva commenced this action asserting breach by Parapluie in failing to pay the proceeds.

Questions

1. What are the best arguments both for Godiva and Parapluie?

2. What is the benefit to insurers in centralizing all of the decision-making in health and life insurance-type cases? How does this differ from the process used in property insurance?

3. Why do conditional receipt cases continue to exist?

4. In a case like this, why does the Insurer return the premium already paid?

5. Would your result change if Agent Helm had told Godiva, after Godiva read the clause requiring Godiva to complete any required medical examination form, "Don't worry, Ellis, you completed the questionnaire--that's all the company means by that statement?"

PROBLEM 23

Assume that in the preceding problem, Ellis Godiva lived. Godiva received a physical examination from a Parapluie-chosen doctor on April 25, 1988. The doctor approved the application for life insurance and a policy was issued and delivered to Godiva on May 14, 1988. Shortly after that policy issued, Godiva completed payment for one full year of life insurance. No further payments were made by Godiva, who tired of the entire idea of life insurance. Godiva died of natural causes on March 15, 1989. Parapluie refused to pay because the policy's one year term ended on February 28, 1989. Discuss.

PROBLEM 24

Having had a bad experience in the Godiva case, PROBLEM 22, the Parapluie Indemnity Company is thinking of changing its Conditional Receipt. This Receipt is used in cases where the applicant for insurance has completed all necessary application forms but where the insurance has not issued because Parapluie has not yet approved the application. In the typical case, the proposed insured would fill out an application, including a brief medical history and pay the first two months premiums. At that point, the Parapluie agent would issue a Conditional Receipt. Parapluie would like to obligate itself to as little as possible by the Conditional Receipt and has shown you, an attorney on its staff, the following forms.[1] Parapluie would like to avoid liability in any case where the applicant applies for insurance, fills out a medical form, does not have a physical exam, and dies before the company rejects the application. Discuss the potential obligations of Parapluie under each of the following:

> A: The Insurance hereby applied for shall not take effect unless the first premium is paid and the policy is delivered to and received by me during my lifetime and good health, and unless

1. These forms are reprinted from R. Keeton & A. Widiss, Insurance Law 55-57 (West, 1988) with permission of West Publishing Co. (footnotes omitted).

otherwise agreed in writing the policy shall then relate back to and take effect as of the date of this application.

B: If the application is approved at the home office of the company, *** the policy will be delivered if the insured is alive on its date of issue; and subject to the same conditions, should the death of the person upon whose life the policy is applied for occur prior to the date of issue of the policy and within eight weeks from the date of such application, the company will, upon surrender of this receipt, pay such amount as would have been due under the terms of the policy had it been issued on the date of such deposit.

C: If the amount of such premium is paid to the said company's agent at the time of making this application, the insurance (subject to the provisions of the said company's regular form of policy for the plan applied for) shall be effective from the date of my medical examination therefor and such a policy shall be issued and delivered to me or my legal representatives, provided the said company in its judgment shall be satisfied as to my insurability, on the plan applied for, on the date of such medical examination; and if said company shall not be so satisfied the amount of the premium paid shall be returned.

D: If the first full premium is paid at the time of making this application, and if at that time the applicant is insurable under the company's rules and practices, for the amount and upon the plan applied for without modification, then the insurance (subject to the provisions of the company's "regular form" of policy for the plan applied for) shall be effective from the time of making application. If the underwriting rules of the company prevent issuance of a policy exactly as applied for but permit issuance on another basis, and the insured dies within sixty days and the issuable policy has neither become effective nor been refused, the insurance shall be in force for such lesser amount as the premium would have purchased when applied as the first premium on the issuable policy.

E. If the first premium is paid at the time of application, the company will be liable from and after said payment to the same extent as if the policy, as applied for, had been issued and delivered at that time; provided, however, that (1) the company reserves the absolute right to reject said application and if said applications is rejected (and without notice thereof) all liability on the part of the company shall thereupon terminate except as to claims maturing before such rejection; and (2) if said application is neither approved nor rejected by the company at its home office within 45 days from the date thereof it shall be deemed to have been rejected as of the last day of such 45 day period, without notice to that effect.

F: If the first premium is paid at the time of making application, the company will make payment in accordance with the terms of the policy applied for, in the event applicant dies on the day of application or within 21 days thereafter.

Problem 25

As attorney for Parapluie Indemnity Company, a health and life insurer, you have been asked for your advice on a relatively new problem. Some courts in states where Parapluie does business have held that payment of premiums in advance is almost certain to create a temporary contract of insurance during the "binder" period, that time in which the company is investigating the risk. As a result, a number of people who are clearly uninsurable because of the advanced stage of some terminal disease have applied for insurance with Parapluie, paid the first two months premium and then died during the investigation period. If Parapluie is held to an insurance contract in the amount applied for, an underwriting disaster is created. You have been asked to study the 6 Conditional Receipts in PROBLEM 24 and the one in PROBLEM 22 and advise if any of them would aid Parapluie in this problem. If not, what do you suggest?

PROBLEM 26

David and Sonya Morgan were getting ready to take a long-planned trip to the Swiss Alps for a skiing vacation and for one semester's study in Geneva. Before they left, they decided to apply for new catastrophic health insurance. On August 6, they met with Nancy Sonnett, their local agent for Mid-Continent Insurance Company and completed an application for Mid-Continent's Major Medical Health Insurance. In the course of filling out the application, Sonya indicated that she once had a very mild, non-recurring heart murmur as an infant. After completing the application and paying the first quarterly premium, the Morgans left Sonnett's office thinking they would be covered after Sonya had a physical examination. The next day, Sonya completed the physical and was advised that she had passed. In fact, however, the Morgans had received a receipt for their check from Mid-Continent, which indicated: "THE INSURANCE APPLIED FOR HEREIN WILL NOT BECOME EFFECTIVE UNTIL THIS APPLICATION HAS BEEN ACCEPTED BY THE HOME OFFICE OF MID-CONTINENT INSURANCE COMPANY."

Several days later, on August 20, the Morgans left for Switzerland. At that time, they were a little surprised that they had heard nothing from Mid-Continent. After they had been in Switzerland for about 2 months, the Morgans still had heard nothing, so Sonya asked her mother during a telephone conversation to check on the policy. Sonya's mother phoned the company directly on October 29 and was told that there had been some problems getting past medical records, but that the problem was resolved. Sonya was involved in an automobile accident in Switzerland on November 17 and required hospitalization. A week later, Mid-Continent gave written notice to the Morgans, in a letter sent to Sonya's Mother, that Mid-Continent would not write the insurance for "health and other reasons." Do the Morgans have any claim to proceeds under this policy?

Notes

E. FISCHER & P. SWISHER, Principles of Insurance Law, Introduction, p. 13; *Hildebrand v. Franklin Life Ins. Co.*, p. 15; notes, p. 21 (Matthew Bender, 1986); R. HENDERSON, Insurance Law, *Statewide Ins. Corp. v. Dewar*, p. 574; notes, p. 582; *Anderson v. Vrahnos*, p. 583; *Keller Lorenz Co. v. Insurance Associates Corp.*, p. 593; *Grandpre v. Northwestern National Life Ins. Co.*, p. 597; *Rohde v. Massachusetts Mut. Life Ins. Co.*, P. 606; notes, pp. 607-608 (Michie, 1989); R. JERRY, Understanding Insurance Law, §33 (Matthew Bender, 1987); R. KEETON & A. WIDISS, Insurance Law, §§2.3(a), (b), (c) (West, 1988); R. KEETON, Basic Insurance Law, *Smith v. Westland Life Ins. Co.*, p. 2; Prudential Ins. Co. v. Lamme, p. 16; *Dunford v. United of Omaha*, p. 39; *New England Mutual Life Ins. Co. v. Hinkle*, p. 44; note & advisory problems, pp. 52 -54; *Duffie v. Bankers' Life Ass'n.*, p. 54; *Zayc v. John Hancock Mutual Life Ins. Co.*, p. 59; *Prudence Mutual Casualty Co. v. Switzer*, p. 73; *Harte v. United Benefit Life Ins. Co.*, p. 551; Harte v. United Benefit Life Ins. Co., p. 555 (West, 1977); A. WIDISS, Insurance, Organization of Marketing, pp. 21-25; *Kleckner v. Mutual Life Ins. Co.*, p. 25; *Puritan Life Ins. Co. v. Guess*, p. 45; *Fields v. Franklin Life Ins. Co.*, p. 58 (West, 1989); K. YORK & J. WHELAN, Insurance Law (Second Edition), *Collister v. Nationwide Life Ins. Co.*, p. 378; note, pp. 389-390; *Rhode v. Massachusetts Mut. Life Ins. Co.*, p. 390; note, pp. 393-94; *Megee v. United States Fidelity & Guaranty Co.*, p. 402; *Friez v. National Old Line Ins. Co.*, p. 404 (West, 1988); W. YOUNG & E. HOLMES, Insurance, *Simses v. North American Co. for Life & Health Ins.*, p. 560; notes, pp. 565-66; The Case of the Banker's Secrets, p. 566; note, p. 567 (Foundation, 1985).

C. Good Faith and Fair Dealing by the Insurance Company

1. The Application Process

(a) Delay

Problem 27

As a professional singer, Gail Phright spent a lot of time traveling. Her recent rock and roll tour, for example, played 60 sites in 65 days. As a result, following her recent second marriage, and because of the continuing growth of her son by a prior marriage, Gail thought she should obtain disability insurance. Gail and her manager applied for disability insurance with Easy Claims Insurance Co through its local agent, Flier Crane. In her application for disability insurance, Gail honestly answered questions about the extent of her travel and lifestyle while on the road. Flier told Gail that he would send the application in to Easy Claims that same day and that he should have an answer for her "in a couple of weeks." Gail's manager indicated that Gail would be away filming a television show for about three weeks but would stop in after that. Almost four weeks later, Gail returned to Flier's office but he was not there. Gail met a secretary, though, who called Easy Claims. The secretary told Gail that Easy Claims was still working on the application, but that they would be done within one week at the latest. The next day, Gail left on an Australian tour with her band. Ten days later, Gail was electrically shocked by defective guitar wiring while performing in Sydney. As a result, Gail remains paralyzed, unable to perform. No disability insurance policy ever issued from Easy Claims. Gail, her husband and son, and her manager have filed suit against Easy Claims in an attempt to obtain the disability insurance payments which, the plaintiffs' claim, Easy Claims has wrongfully withheld.

Questions

1. What is the legal theory under which this claim is filed? Contract? Tort? What elements must be proved?

2. Is it reasonable for Gail, or the other plaintiffs, to expect coverage in this case?

3. Suppose it is shown that Gail had applications pending with other Disability Insurance Companies, but withdrew those applications after applying to Easy Claims. Does this change any of your answers? How?

4. Suppose Gail had paid the first year's premium at the time of the application. Does this change any of your answers? How?

Notes

E. FISCHER & P. SWISHER, Principles of Insurance Law, Introduction, p. 22; *Antoine v. Sentry Life Ins. Co.*, p. 22; notes & questions, pp. 25-26 (Matthew Bender, 1986); R. HENDERSON, Insurance Law, *Continental Life & Acc. Co. v. Songer*, p. 587 (Michie, 1989); R. JERRY, Understanding Insurance Law, §32[a] (Matthew Bender, 1987); R. KEETON & A. WIDISS, Insurance Law, §2.4 (West, 1988); R. KEETON, Basic Insurance Law, *Duffie v. Bankers' Life Ass'n.*, p. 54; Excerpts, p. 60; notes, pp. 60-61 (West, 1977); A. WIDISS, Insurance, *Worden v. Farmers State Co., Inc.*, p. 62; Theoretical Bases for Requiring an Insurer to Act on Applications, p. 66 (West, 1989); K. YORK & J. WHELAN, Insurance Law (Second Edition), *Talbot v. Country Life Insurance Co.*, p. 77 (West, 1988); W. YOUNG & E. HOLMES, Insurance, Delay in Processing Applications, p. 567 (Foundation, 1985).

(b) Rejection of Applications

Problem 28

Henry Steele sought to purchase a new policy of automobile insurance from his local Statewide Insurance Co. agent, Adrian LaRue. Steele indicated that he needed insurance immediately and, as a result, Adrian took his application for insurance, and the first two months premium of $100, which the company required. Adrian indicated that while she could not write insurance for first time Statewide Insurance customers, she could issue a Temporary Binder which would provide insurance for up to 30 days, or until Statewide ruled on the application. Adrian sent the application and check to Statewide, who deposited the check and began its background check on Steele. Two days later, the check was returned from the bank, marked "Insufficient Funds." Statewide then immediately wrote to Steele that his application was rejected because he had not paid the first two months premium as required. This letter arrived at Steele's house two days after Steele caused a serious automobile accident.

Questions

1. Statewide has refused to defend Steele in the automobile accident case claiming that the application was rejected before the accident. What result? Why?

2. Assume that Steele did receive the letter from Statewide on the

same day as the accident. What argument can be made for insurance coverage from Statewide?

3. Assume that Statewide resubmitted Steele's check, that it was honored, but the background check of Steele's driving record showed that Steele had numerous fault accidents. As a result, Statewide refused to write the insurance and allowed the binder to expire. On the 33d day after Steele's receipt of the binder, Steele had the accident.

Notes

R. JERRY, Understanding Insurance Law, §62A[b] (Matthew Bender, 1987); R. KEETON & A. WIDISS, Insurance Law, §2.4 (West, 1988); R. KEETON, Basic Insurance Law, *Smith v. Westland Life Ins. Co.*, p. 2; *Prudential Ins. Co. v. Lamme*, p. 16 (West, 1977); A. WIDISS, Insurance, *Collister v. Nationwide Ins. Co.*, p. 6; *Knievel v. Fidelity Marketing Corp.*, p. 633 (West, 1989); K. YORK & J. WHELAN, Insurance Law (Second Edition), The Policy Has Been Cancelled, p. 282; *Collister v. Nationwide Life Ins. Co.*, p. 378 (West, 1988).

(c) Counteroffers

Problem 29

Perfect Insurance Company has sued Edie Vernon for past due amounts of $450 which Perfect claims is due on a liability insurance policy written on a bar owned by Edie. Edie went to Perfect and sought liability insurance coverage for the bar and was quoted a price of $500 for the first 3 months of coverage. Edie paid that amount and received a binder covering the bar for liability while Perfect investigated the risk. When it did so, Perfect found that Edie had experienced two recent claims for selling liquor to underage persons.

As a result, Perfect was willing to issue the insurance only for an increased premium of $950 every three months. It sent this information to Edie in a letter which Edie received. Thereafter, Edie did nothing more. Perfect has now filed suit for the remainder of $450 on the three months coverage and Edie has counterclaimed for that portion of the original $500 which was not used in providing coverage between the time that Edie received Perfect's letter and the end of three months. Who wins?

Notes

R. KEETON & A. WIDISS, Insurance Law, §2.1(c)(1) (West, 1988); R. KEETON, Basic Insurance Law, *Dunford v. United of Omaha*, p. 39 (West, 1977).

2. Collection of Premiums

Problem 30

Robert Arends had a flood insurance policy with Federal Fidelity and Liability Insurance Co. which would pay for damage to Arends' business property as a result of flood. The premium on the policy was paid by Arends on a semi-annual basis on July 1 and December 1. The policy provided:

> PAYMENT OF PREMIUMS: Premiums hereunder are to be received by the company at its home office not later than the 1st day of July and the 1st day of December in each and every year in which this policy is in force. In the event the company elects to receive premium payment hereunder at any other time or in any other location, any such election shall not amount to a waiver by the company of the requirements of this paragraph.

Beginning with the third premium, Arends made payments increasingly late. During the first three years, his premiums were paid on December 10, July 4, December 9, July 12, December 3, July 10. On each of these occasions, Arends received a receipt of his premium payment from the company and an acknowledgement that his premiums were paid up to date. On December 4, of the fourth year of the policy, a flood severely damaged Arend's business. Federal Fidelity and Liability has refused to pay on this loss, claiming that the insurance coverage expired when Arends failed to make payment on December 1 as required.

Questions

1. Discuss Arend's best argument(s) for coverage under the facts.

2. Assume that Federal Fidelity received Arend's premium payment after notifying Arends of the cancellation of the policy for failure to pay, but before Federal Fidelity learned of the loss. If the premium is then accepted, will the loss be covered?

3. Assume that Federal had not cancelled Arends' insurance for failure to pay on December 1, but did so after it learned of the loss. Does your theory of liability change? How?

Problem 31

Joan Stone suffered over $50,000 worth of damage when her home burned on December 23. When she reported this loss to BPA Insurance Co., who Joan thought held her fire insurance, she learned for the first time that the company claimed there was no coverage. The policy had originally been purchased by Joan on December 17, three years ago. On the first renewal date, Joan failed to pay the premium before December 17; in fact, it was paid on December 19. On the second renewal date, the premium was paid on December 23. On the third renewal, the premium was paid on December 26 of the year before the fire took place. The policy itself provides as follows:

> EFFECTIVE DATE--This policy shall be in effect from 12:00 noon on December 17, and shall remain in effect until 12:00 noon on the next succeeding December 17.
>
> ***
>
> TERMINATION--This policy shall automatically terminate if a renewal premium is not paid at the home office of the company prior to the expiration date of the then current term.

Joan acknowledges that she did not pay the premium that the company claims was due prior to December 17 of the year of the fire, however, she argues that she thought, reasonably, that there was coverage on the date of the fire. How can this argument be legally made?

Notes

E. FISCHER & P. SWISHER, Principles of Insurance Law, *Life Ins. Co. of the Southwest v. Overstreet*, p. 39; notes & questions, pp. 43-44; "Grace Period"--Introduction, p. 45; *Brand v. Monumental Life Ins. Co.*, p. 46; notes & questions, pp. 47-48 (Matthew Bender, 1986); R. JERRY, Understanding Insurance Law, §71[c], [e] (Matthew Bender, 1987); R. KEETON & A. WIDISS, Insurance Law, §6.8(c) (West, 1988); R. KEETON, Basic Insurance Law, *Barnett v. State Auto & Cas. Underwriters*, p. 623; *Seavey v. Erickson*, p. 744; *Southland Life Ins. Co. v. Lawson*, p. 749 (West, 1977); A. WIDISS, Insurance, *Life Ins. Co. of the Southwest v. Overstreet*, p. 560; *Brand v. Monumental Life Ins. Co.*, p. 566 (West, 1989); K. YORK & J. WHELAN, Insurance Law (Second Edition), Note, Waiver, Estoppel, Etc.--A Comment, pp. 85-86; note, pp. 86-87 (West, 1988).

3. Cancellation

Problem 32

Robert and Jane Armstrong had automobile insurance with Safety First Insurance Company for 6 years prior to November 15 of last year. The policy had been renewed every 6 months without difficulty. In early October of last year, however, the Armstrongs received a letter from Safety First telling them that their policy would not be renewed on November 15 because of "claims frequency and an unrevealed speeding ticket for doing 65 mph in a 55 mph zone." Following this letter, the Armstrongs sought insurance with other insurers but found that they would be placed in the "high risk" classification as a result of the non-renewal by Safety First. As a result, Robert Armstrong sought information from Safety First about why the Armstrongs were not renewed. In response to his letter, Mr. Armstrong received an itemized list of claims which had been made:

> 1. June, 8 years ago--Comprehensive claim--rock from another auto broke windshield;
>
> 2. January, 6 years ago--Collision claim--car was stolen and damaged in accident;
>
> 3. December, 6 years ago--Liability--Other driver ran stop sign and sued insured for injuries. Case was dismissed although Safety First paid a collision claim for damage to Insured's car;

4. February, 4 years ago--Comprehensive claim--tires slashed in a parking lot;

5. April, 4 years ago--Collision Claim--Insured's car struck by another car.

Mr. Armstrong admits that he received the speeding ticket, but after he did, Safety First did not inquire about it at the next renewal time; rather, the Armstrongs simply received the policy in the mail.

State statute does not forbid insurers from cancelling automobile policies, but provides that the company must provide the insured with "the actual reason" for non-renewal. The Armstrongs have hired you to investigate whether they have any legal action which they can file against Safety First. What are your best arguments?

Problem 33

When she forgot to pay the March installment on her automobile insurance premium on time, Margaret Hopping's automobile insurance company, The Equity Group, sent her a notice indicating that the insurance was cancelled, effective on March 31, because of Margaret's consistent failure to pay the semi-monthly installments on time. On April 1, Margaret remembered that she forgot to pay the March installment, and called her local agent, who told her to just put the money in the mail to the company. Margaret mailed her check on April 3, and it was received on April 6. Margaret was involved in an accident on April 5 and the company has told her that it will not pay on her claim because the insurance was cancelled pursuant to the policy. The policy provided for cancellation on the basis of non-payment of a premium installment so long as the company:

> [M]ailed to the named insured at the address shown in the policy written notice stating when not less than ten days thereafter such cancellation shall be effective. The mailing of notice as aforesaid shall be sufficient proof of notice.

Margaret has filed suit against The Equity Group to declare that the policy was not effectively cancelled.

Questions

1. Who bears the risk of non-persuasion on the issue of cancellation?

2. After The Equity Group proves that the Notice of Cancellation was mailed, Margaret tries to offer evidence that she did not receive the notice. Must this evidence be admitted? How must notice be mailed?

3. If the Court admits the evidence that Margaret did not receive the notice, can The Equity Group introduce rebuttal evidence to show that the notice was sent to Margaret's last known address, and that it came back to The Equity Group with the notation "Moved; Left No Forwarding Address?"

4. What do state statutes in your state provide regarding these issues?

Notes

E. FISCHER & P. SWISHER, Principles of Insurance Law, "Renewal and Cancellation," Introduction; *King v. Guardian Life Ins. Co.*, p. 63; notes & questions, pp. 66-67; *National Automobile & Cas. Ins. Co. v. California Cas. Ins. Co.*, p. 67 (Matthew Bender, 1986); R. HENDERSON, Insurance Law, *Markel v. Travelers Ins. Co.*, p. 617; notes, p. 622; *Guardian Life Ins. Co. of America v. Zerance*, p. 622; *Edens v. South Carolina Farm Bureau Mut. Ins. Co.*, p. 640; *Government Employees Ins. Co. v. Superior Court*, p. 643 (Michie, 1989); R. JERRY, Understanding Insurance Law, §62A[c] (Matthew Bender, 1987); R. KEETON & A. WIDISS, §5.11 (West, 1988); R. KEETON, Basic Insurance Law, *Merchants & Farmers Mut. Cas. Co. v. St. Paul-Mercury Indemnity Co.*, p. 575; *Donarski v. Lardy*, p. 577; *Seavey v. Erickson*, p.

744 (West, 1977); K. YORK & J. WHELAN, Insurance Law (Second Edition), Note, That the Policy Has Been Cancelled (With or Without Cause), pp. 282-285 (West, 1988).

D. Insurance Agent and Broker Problems

1. Licensing

Problem 34

Yesterday, a high school classmate of yours, Gerry Appleton, called you at your office and asked for your help. Appleton, who had been a salesperson for a now out-of-business car dealership, had been contacted by Golden Plus Insurance Company, a multiple lines insurance company in your state. Golden Plus had heard of Appleton's success in sales and wanted Appleton to set up a local Insurance Agency which would sell the Golden Plus line of insurance. After some negotiation, Appleton was able to get Golden Plus to allow Appleton to sell other company's lines of insurance as well. In addition, Appleton thought that the agency could employ some persons who would simply make themselves available to clients for the purpose of soliciting quotes from insurance carriers for still further types of insurance.

In seeking your help, Appleton, a college graduate who has no formal training in insurance, has several questions for which answers are sought under your own state's insurance laws:

Questions

1. Are there any special requirements for setting up an Insurance Agency? What are they?

2. What qualifications will Appleton need to meet in order to obtain a license as an Insurance Agent?

3. Under what circumstances can that license be taken away? By whom? Under what process?

4. Appleton is thinking about becoming "Exclusive Agent" for Golden Plus Insurance Company. Does that title have any special significance?

5. Do the people whom Appleton will hire to solicit insurance company bids for insurance for clients of the agency need any special license? What are the requirements? How can that license be removed?

6. Appleton has a friend in an adjoining state who also owns an insurance agency. Because of the number of businesses which do business in both states, Appleton is thinking about combining forces with the other agency and would like to know how the agents in this state can be licensed in the adjoining state and vice versa?

Notes

R. KEETON & A. WIDISS, Insurance Law, §§2.5, 8.2(b) (West, 1988); R. KEETON, Basic Insurance Law, *Department of Ins. v. Motor Ins. Corp.*, 968-974 (West, 1977); K. YORK & J. WHELAN, Insurance Law (Second Edition), *Washington Nat. Ins. v. Strickland* 73-77 (West, 1988).

2. Actual Authority of Agent/Broker

Problem 35

Luther Bouse had a contract with Mutual Insurance Company, which allowed Bouse:

> [T]o solicit applications for insurance, collect initial premiums and remit company owned money to the company in the manner and at such times as may be prescribed by the company, and, while in possession of any such money, to hold it in trust as the absolute property of the company; to reinstate and transfer insurance; report, investigate and handle losses and claims under the company's directions ***.

Bouse first met Daniel and Claudette Gruver when they came to Bouse's office for property insurance on their trailer. Bouse, who knew that Mutual would not write trailer insurance unless there was evidence that the trailer was anchored to the ground, nonetheless took the Gruver's application and money and told them that they would be covered unless they heard otherwise from him. The next day, Bouse visited the trailer and discovered that it was not anchored. Bouse filed this report with Mutual and sought instructions on whether a policy would issue. Before those instructions were issued, the Gruver's trailer was ruined by fire. After Mutual denied any liability for the loss, the Gruver's sued Mutual and obtained a judgement for the face value of the policy they had requested--$40,000. Following that verdict, Mutual has sought judgment against Bouse for the same amount.

Questions

1. Did Bouse have Actual Authority to bind Mutual to a contract of oral insurance for Gruver?

2. If Bouse had no Actual Authority, can Bouse be liable to Mutual for the amount of the Gruver judgment?

3. If Bouse had no Actual Authority, how can Mutual be liable on the claim?

4. If Bouse was found by the court to have had Apparent Authority, how does this change the claim by Mutual against Bouse for breach of Actual Authority?

Notes

E. FISCHER & P. SWISHER, Principles of Insurance Law, *Gulf Ins. Co. v. Grisham*, p. 9; notes & questions, p. 12; Contractual Powers of Insurance Agents, p. 26; *Weaver v. Metropolitan Life Ins. Co.*, p. 27; notes & questions, p. 29 (Matthew Bender, 1986); R. JERRY, Understanding Insurance Law, §§35[a], [b] (Matthew Bender, 1987); R. KEETON & A. WIDISS, Insurance Law, §§2.5(b)(4) (West, 1988); R. KEETON, Basic Insurance Law, Excerpts, pp. 66-67 (West, 1977).

Problem 36

The Arcadia Valley Insurance Agency had a contract with East Coast Fidelity Insurance Company which permitted Arcadia Valley "to receive and accept proposals for fire insurance with East Coast Fidelity Insurance Company." In accordance with that contract, Arcadia's manager wrote fire insurance for William and Joanne Morris for their home for a period of one year. At that time, the premium was paid in full, but Arcadia's manager forgot to prepare renewal cards--cards which would be sent to the insurance company and prompt the writing of a new policy at the renewal date. Just before the year was about to run out, Mr. and Mrs. Morris contacted Arcadia about a renewal and spoke with the same manager. The manager authorized renewal, collected the money from Mr. and Mrs. Morris, and forwarded the papers on to East Coast. Because there was no renewal card, however, the policy did not issue. Fire destroyed the Morris home thirty days after the original policy had expired. In an action against East Coast, Mr. and Mrs. Morris proved that Arcadia was the agent of the company and had authority to write renewal policies. As a result, Mr. and Mrs. Morris were able to collect the full amount of insurance, $75,000, which had originally been written on the house. Thereafter, East Coast sued Arcadia for Arcadia's negligence in failing to send in renewal cards which caused the company to miss renewing the Morris policy. In that suit, what specifically must East Coast prove?

Notes

R. JERRY, Understanding Insurance Law, §35[c][1] (Matthew Bender, 1987); R. KEETON & A. WIDISS, Insurance Law, §§2.5(a), 2.5(b)(4)(i) (West, 1988); R. KEETON, Basic Insurance Law, *Julien v. Spring Lake Park Agency, Inc.*, p. 67; *Nelson v. Glens Falls Ins. Co.*, p. 70 (West, 1977); K. YORK & J. WHELAN, Insurance Law (Second Edition), *Washington National Insurance Co. v. Strickland*, p. 73 (West, 1988).

3. Apparent Authority

(a) Regarding the Insurance Policy

Problem 37

When they needed financing to buy their home, Michael and Arlene Philips went to Sam Berends, the loan officer of Northeast Land Bank. Berends approved the loan and inquired of the Philips if they wanted credit life insurance. Berends indicated that Northeast had a working relationship with Alberta Mutual Life whereby bank officers would offer Alberta Mutual credit life, and Alberta would attempt to keep premium requirements to a minimum. In fact, the agreement between Northeast and Alberta allowed loan officers of Northeast to:

1. offer to sell Alberta Mutual credit life;
2. take insurance applications from borrowers;
3. send out promotional literature about Alberta Mutual in connection with other bank mailings;
4. serve as contact persons for borrowers who had purchased credit life with Alberta Mutual and who had questions;
5. receive and file claims from Alberta Mutual insureds.

When Michael and Arlene Philips closed their loan with Northeast Land Bank, Berends went over the application from Alberta with them. That application asked a number of medical questions and Berends went over with Michael and Arlene the process that would be used to determine if the Philips were insurable. While their application was pending, Berends encouraged the Philips to fill out a second Alberta Mutual application for Temporary Insurance. That Temporary Insurance would be immediately effective and would last for a period of 75 days (unless a permanent application was sooner accepted or rejected by the company) if the first premium was paid and all questions on the application for Temporary Insurance were answered. The Phillips answered all questions, paid the first premium, and asked Berends: "Will we be notified when the Temporary Insurance is ready to run out? With working on our new house, we are likely to forget." Berends indicated: "You should be notified." During the next 75 days, the Phillips received several inquiries from Alberta Mutual about the permanent insurance and Michael Phillips was asked to take a physical examination. None of these inquiries mentioned any expiration time for the Temporary Insurance. 85 days after the loan closed, Michael Phillips was killed in an automobile accident. Alberta had already sent, the day before Michael Phillips' death, rejection of the permanent insurance, because of several disclosed health problems suffered by Michael. After his death, Alberta refused to pay on the Temporary Insurance, claiming that it had run out at the end of 75 days. Arlene Phillips has claimed that Berends had the authority to modify the contract for Temporary Insurance so as to require notice of termination of that coverage. Berends has indicated that he knew that neither he, nor any officer of Northeast, had the power to make decisions to accept or reject insurance or to vary the terms of any insurance offered by Alberta Mutual. The case is now at trial.

Questions

1. Does Northeast Land Bank, through its loan officers, have actual authority to extend the 75 day provision?

2. How would a contract for insurance arise between Phillips and Alberta Mutual for any period beyond the 75 day term of Temporary Insurance?

3. How could it be found that Berends (or any other loan officer of Northeast) obtained authority from Alberta to orally modify in the face of Berends admission that he knew that he had no such authority?

4. If Apparent Authority is to exist, to whom must it be communicated?

5. How will Arlene Phillips best argue that apparent authority was communicated in this case?

6. If Alberta Mutual is required to pay a death benefit to Arlene Phillips, does it have any action against Northeast Land Bank?

PROBLEM 38

George Webber, a wounded Vietnam veteran, applied for a decreasing term life insurance policy with Citylife Insurance Co. Because Webber had been wounded, indeed declared 75% disabled by the Veteran's Administration, Webber told Clayton Maddox, the agent with whom Webber dealt, that Webber wanted a "waiver of premium" provision in the policy. Under that provision, premiums would be waived in the event of the disability of the insured. After completing the application, Webber passed it along to Citylife which immediately issued a life policy to Webber without the waiver of premium feature. When Webber received that policy, he immediately contacted Maddox and sought to reapply for a life policy with waiver of premium provisions. At the time, Webber advised Maddox that he had to have surgery in a month and would, in fact, be out of work for several months thereafter. While Webber filled out the second application, Maddox assured him that the price that Maddox was using for the premiums was the price that would be applicable for a decreasing term life policy with waiver of premiums for a person Webber's age. Maddox arrived at this figure by using "sales brochures" sent to him by Citylife Insurance Company which clearly indicated "CITYLIFE, your Whole Life Company" on the cover. Thus, Webber was not concerned that the application itself made no reference to waiver of premium. Webber paid the premium for the first six months of the policy with the application and authorized monthly deductions from his bank account for the months thereafter. When the second policy arrived, Webber quickly scanned it to see if it contained a waiver of premiums provision. He was unconcerned, however, that it did not because there was no return of any premium to him, which Maddox had assured Webber would occur if the company rejected the waiver of premiums provisions. Seven months later, Webber became disabled and, to conserve finances, authorized his bank to discontinue payments to Citylife. Three months later, Webber died. Citylife acknowledges that Webber would have been considered disabled within the meaning of a waiver of premiums provision, but denies that one existed. Citylife also indicates that it would never have written a waiver of premium policy for Webber because of his physical condition. Citylife has a contract with Clayton Maddox making him a "Soliciting Agent Only," and expressly denying him the power to negotiate beyond the terms of any Citylife policy. As attorney for the Estate of George Webber, how will you defeat the claim that the policy lapsed for failure to pay the premium (a permissible practice in the state)?

PROBLEM 39

In conjunction with her dealership's sale of new cars, Sue Tanner, the Finance Manager at Trader Dave's New and Used Car Sales, had been persuaded by South County Life Insurance to solicit credit life insurance policies for South County in connection with car loans financed through Third State Bank. As a result, when Arnold Caves sought to purchase a new car from Trader Dave, Sue Tanner asked Caves if he wanted credit life insurance through South County Life. When Caves said yes, Tanner simply checked the box on the loan application. Tanner did not ask any physical or mental history questions, as she was not supposed to do so pursuant to her agreement with South County Life. South County did not require any written application and had issued policies to anyone with whom Sue Tanner made the appropriate financing arrangements. South County provided no guidance to Tanner on whom to approve or reject. In that regard, the amount of the premium for the credit life was calculated and added in to the base cost of the loan to figure the monthly payment. Insurance was effective upon approval of the loan. Caves received a monthly payment book for that amount. In the copy of the loan application, near the box for credit life was the statement: "As a condition of this insurance, the insured must be in insurable health at the time this policy was written. Please refer to Master Policy for details." Neither Tanner nor Caves ever saw a Master Policy. Caves had a history of heart disease and heart attack. He died before making a payment on the approved loan. South County claims that Tanner was a soliciting agent only and had no power to bind the company to insurance. How should the Caves Estate argue in rebuttal?

Notes

E. FISCHER & P. SWISHER, Principles of Insurance Law, *Gulf Ins. Co. v. Grisham*, p. 9; notes & questions, p. 12; Contractual Powers of Insurance Agents, p. 26; *Weaver v. Metropolitan Life Ins. Co.*, p. 27; notes & questions, p. 29 (Matthew Bender, 1986); R. JERRY, Understanding Insurance Law, §§35[b], [d] (Matthew Bender, 1987); R. KEETON & A. WIDISS, Insurance Law, §§2.5(b)(4)(ii), 2.5(c)(1)&(2), 2.5(d) (West, 1988); R. KEETON, Basic Insurance Law, *Gulbrandson v. Empire Mutual Ins. Co.*, p. 19; *Milwaukee Bedding Co. v. Graebner*, p. 62; *Prudence Mutual Casualty Co. v. Switzer*, p. 73; *Barnett v. State Auto & Casualty Underwriters*, p. 623 (West, 1977); K. YORK & J. WHELAN, Insurance Law (Second Edition), Note, Methods of Marketing Insurance, pp. 67-68; *Washington National Ins. Co. v. Strickland*, p. 73 (West, 1988); W. YOUNG & E. HOLMES, Insurance, *Hayat Carpet Cleaning Co., Inc. v. Northern Assurance Co., Ltd., of London*, p. 207 (Foundation, 1985).

(b) As to Waiver or Estoppel Regarding Company Rights

Problem 40

Layton Bell owned a commercial building insured by Regional Security Property and Casualty Co. That insurance was purchased through Julia Roper of the J.L. Roper & Associates Insurance Agency. The Roper agency has signs from Regional Security Property and Casualty, as well as several other property insurance companies, hanging on the wall. The stationery for the J.L. Roper & Assoc. agency has "Independent Insurance Agents" emblazoned on it. When Bell purchased the insurance, Julia Roper gave him a pen and calendar containing the familiar blue police car with the words "Regional Security" printed on it, a symbol well-known as that of Regional Security Property and Casualty. The calendar also had "J.L. Roper & Assoc." printed under the Regional Security name.

Several years after purchasing the commercial building, Bell agreed to sell it to Oliver & Cathy Reeves. As a result, Bell, who had just paid the full year's premium on his property insurance policy with Regional Security, asked Julia Roper if the property insurance could be transferred to the new owner. Julia indicated that it could and that the Reeves would not owe additional money until the following year's premium was due. The land transfer was made and three months later, the property burned to the ground. When Bell went to the Roper agency to make a claim, however, he was advised that there was no insurance on the property because it had been sold. Upon checking the policy, Bell found the language: "This policy shall terminate upon transfer of the property to one other than the insured."

Questions

1. You represent Mr. and Mrs. Reeves and would like to prove that Roper had the power to permit transfer of the policy. What evidence can you produce?

2. How would your case be helped if your state had the following statute:

> Every person who solicits insurance on behalf of any insurance company or takes or transmits, other than for himself, an application for insurance or a policy of insurance *** shall be held to be an agent of the company for which the act is done or the risk is taken, whether any of such acts shall be done at the instance or request or by the employment of the insurance company ***.

Notes

E. FISCHER & P. SWISHER, Principles of Insurance Law, Contractual Powers of Insurance Agent, p. 26; *Weaver v. Metropolitan Life Ins. Co.*, p. 27; notes & questions, p. 29 (Matthew Bender, 1986); R. HENDERSON, Insurance Law, *Republic Ins. Co. v. Silverton Elevators, Inc.*, p. 778; notes, pp. 787-790 (Michie, 1989); R. JERRY, Understanding Insurance Law, §§35[b], [d] (Matthew Bender, 1987); R. KEETON & A. WIDISS, Insurance Law, §§6.1(b)(3), 6.8(a), 6.8(d) (West, 1988); R. KEETON, Basic Insurance Law, *Republic Ins. Co. v. Silverton Elevators, Inc.*, p. 715, *State Farm Fire Ins. Co. v. Rakes*, p. 726 (West, 1977); K. YORK & J. WHELAN, Insurance Law (Second Edition), Note, Waiver, Estoppel, Etc.--A Comment, pp. 85-86; *Republic Insurance Co. v. Silverton Elevators, Inc.*, p. 87; problem, p. 91; *Tate v. Charles Aguillard Insurance & Real Estate, Inc.*, p. 91 (West, 1988).

(c) As to Payment of Premiums

Problem 41

When Robert Kirkland purchased a policy of homeowner's insurance from The Underwriter's Group for his new home, he dealt with Linda Witman of the Linda Witman Agency. Kirkland, who did not have very much money because of the initial closing costs on this home, asked Linda to arrange for financing of the premiums which she did through Capital Premium Financing, Inc. After the policy had initially issued, an investigator for The Underwriters Group visited the home and determined that its value was well in excess of the insurance purchased so that additional insurance was required. Robert Kirkland told Linda to arrange for this additional insurance, but that he would not have any money to pay for it other than as previously financed. Linda Witman arranged for a new policy to issue, arranged to have the previously issued policy cancelled, and arranged to have the unused premium then accrued on the existing policy serve as a down payment on the new policy, the balance of which would be financed. At this time, The Underwriters changed their billing practices and advised agents not to send in down payments on new insurance, but rather await billing direct from the company. Linda did this on the Kirkland policy, as well as others. Thereafter, Kirkland received notice that the new policy was to be cancelled for non-payment of premium. When he called Linda, she indicated that she would take care of it and that he need not worry because she had just received the prior unearned premium and had instructed her secretary to hold it pending arrival of a bill from The Underwriters Group. Several weeks later, Kirkland's home burned to the ground. The Underwriters Group took the position that the policy had been cancelled for non-payment of premium. An underwriter for The Underwriters indicated that the Kirkland policy was considered a renewal and not new insurance and thus, when no money was sent in with the application, and none was thereafter immediately forthcoming, the insurance was cancelled.

Questions

1. Kirkland wishes to sue The Underwriters Group and claim that the insurance was in effect on his property as a result of the statements made by Linda Witman. The Underwriters Group has taken the position that its contract with its agents forbids the agent from waiving any payment of premium provisions. Linda has agreed that this language is in her agreement with The Underwriters Group. Can Kirkland win based upon apparent authority?

2. How does the case change if state statute provides:

> Any person who shall act as agent for any insurance company within this state, or who shall, as agent, solicit applications,

> deliver policies or renewal receipts and collect premiums thereon, or who shall receive or collect moneys from any source or on any account whatsoever, as agent, for any insurance company shall be responsible in a trust or fiduciary capacity to the company for any money so collected or received.

Notes

R. KEETON & A. WIDISS, Insurance Law, §6.8(c) (West, 1988); R. KEETON, Basic Insurance Law, *Seavey v. Erickson*, p. 744; *Southland Life Ins. Co. v. Lawson*, p. 749 (West, 1977).

(d) Authority for Dishonest Conduct

Problem 42

Agent Eddie Arent, recently inducted into the Safe Family Insurance Company's "Million Dollar Sales Club," met his long-time friend Arnold DeFea for coffee. DeFea had life, health, and property insurance with various companies, but all purchased through Arent. At coffee, Eddie told DeFea: "Arnold, your homeowners with Safe Family is about to be up for renewal--how about if I come out to the house, make sure nothing has changed, and we rewrite the policy?" DeFea immediately agreed. The next evening, Arent arrived at the DeFea home, reviewed the floor plans, made some notes on various items of personal property contained in the house, and asked a few questions about home storage of valuables. As he was leaving, Arent asked if DeFea would like to accompany Arent and some other Safe Family agents on a weekend fishing trip. DeFea declined, stating that he was taking his entire family on a weekend camping trip. The DeFea home was burglarized while the DeFeas were on their camping trip. Suspicion soon focused on Eddie Arent who ultimately confessed to the burglary of the DeFea home (as well as several others). While Safe Family paid the DeFea's insurance claim for the personal property which was fenced by Eddie before his arrest, the DeFea's have contacted you about possible civil suit against Safe Family for trespass, conversion and punitive damages. Can such a theory be successful?

(e) Authority in Group Insurance

Problem 43

As part of her employment as a Strickland University professor, Annette Freund is covered by College Lines Group Health Insurance. That insurance is administered by the Strickland University Employee Benefits Office, whose employees are all regular Strickland University staff members. When Annette joined the faculty, she went to the Employee Benefits Office to fill out the application form for health insurance and was helped in that regard by Mabel Lawe, who appeared to be an employee. Later letters from Lawes to Annette revealed that Lawe was Plan Administrator for University Insurance. Lawes answered questions about coverage for Annette; indicated the extent of employee contribution to premiums and showed Annette the Master Policy of group health insurance. Lawes indicated that individual employees would not receive this policy, but would receive a summary of benefits prepared with College Life by the Benefits Office. After receiving her summary of benefits,

Annette called the Benefits Office and spoke with Mabel Lawes about the extent of coverage in the Strickland University Medical Center as opposed to similar coverage in a local private hospital. Mabel assured Annette that the coverages were the same. Thus, when Annette had to select a hospital for delivery of her first baby, she choose a private hospital near her doctor's office. When she received a statement from College Life regarding payment of her labor, delivery, and infant care charges, however, Annette discovered that she was reimbursed for only 75% of the charges in a private hospital, as opposed to the 90% reimbursement she would have received if she had gone to the Strickland University Medical Center. Annette's research also revealed that her overall charges at the Strickland University Medical Center would have been virtually identical to those she incurred at the private hospital. When she went to the Employee Benefit Office and reviewed the Master Policy with Mabel Lawes, Annette found that the policy only paid 75% of those charges for private hospitals, unless use of the private hospital was approved by College Life prior to the charge.

Questions

1. Based upon traditional concepts of Apparent Authority, can Annette succeed in proving that Mabel Lawes had the authority from College Life to approve the private hospital?

2. What difference exists in the relationship between Mabel Lawes and Annette that does not exist in other Agent/Insured cases? Do University employees benefit from any such differences? How?

3. Will Annette be able to successfully argue that College Life has pre-

agreed to the private hospital, based upon Mabel's statements?

Notes

R. JERRY, Understanding Insurance Law, §121 (Matthew Bender, 1987); R. KEETON & A. WIDISS, Insurance Law, §2.6 (West, 1988); R. KEETON, Basic Insurance Law, *Ogden v. Continental Casualty Co.*, p. 82; *Magee v. Equitable Life Assurance Society*, p. 87; *All States Life Ins. Co. v. Tillman*, p. 89; *Gilford v. Emergency Aid Ins. Co.*, p. 89 (West, 1977); K. YORK & J. WHELAN, Insurance Law (Second Edition), Note, Group-Insurance Marketing, pp. 68-70 (West, 1988).

E. Direct Duty of Agent/Broker to Insured

Problem 44

The facts in this problem are the same as those in *Estate of George Webber v. Citylife Insurance Co.*, Problem 38.

Questions

1. As trial of the case gets closer, you, as attorney for the Estate become more worried about the ability to prove that Clayton Maddox had apparent authority from Citylife to obligate Citylife to a waiver of premiums. The time for amending your pleadings has not yet expired. Is there any direct action against Maddox which should be pursued?

2. If you do file suit directly against Maddox, what will be his best defense?

3. Assume that the case is tried to a jury and that the jury finds Citylife liable based upon apparent authority and also finds George Maddox liable in the direct action which you added against him. Do you have any concerns?

PROBLEM 45

The facts in this problem are the same as those in *Layton Bell, et als. v. National Security Property and Casualty Co.*, PROBLEM 40.

Questions

1. Prior to trial, you amend your pleadings to add a count for breach of the duty to procure against J.L. Roper & Associates. What are the elements of that action and how will they be pleaded?

2. What are the damages?

Notes

E. FISCHER & P. SWISHER, Principles of Insurance Law, Notes & questions, p. 29 (Matthew Bender, 1986); R. HENDERSON, Insurance Law, *Keller Lorenz Co. v. Insurance Associates Corp*, p. 593; notes, p. 597 (Michie, 1989); R. JERRY, Understanding Insurance Law, §§35[c][2][i], [ii] (Matthew Bender, 1987); R. KEETON & A. WIDISS, Insurance Law, §2.5(c)(3) (West, 1988); R. KEETON, Basic Insurance Law, *Julien v. Spring Lake Park Agency, Inc.*, p. 67; *Nelson v. Glens Falls Ins. Co.*, p. 70; *Boston Camping Distributor Co. v. Lumbermens Mutual Cas. Co.*, p. 72 (West, 1977); K. YORK & J. WHELAN, Insurance Law (Second Edition), *Maryland Casualty Co. v. J.M. Foster*, p. 79; note, p. 82 (West, 1988).

Chapter Five

Property Insurance

A. Insurable Interest

Problem 46

Wee Willie Caufield, after 15 years as a thoroughbred race horse jockey, finally got to ride a champion. Citator, a two-year-old mare from Apple Down Stables who had not done well in early races, responded magnificently when Caufield took the reins. After breezing to victory in his first two races on Citator, Caufield was offered an exclusive contract by Apple Down to ride Citator. Caufield was guaranteed $30,000 over a three year period to ride Citator in the remaining 5 two-year-old stakes races, as well as the 3 Triple Crown three-year-old races and 7 other three-year-old stakes races. In addition to salary, Caufield's agreement called for him to receive "the usual percentage" of purse winnings. As the jockey's usual percentage was 10% of the purse, this additional compensation could make Caufield a wealthy man. Because of the uncertainties normally associated with horse racing, Caufield has sought to purchase an insurance policy on Citator, so as to protect both his guaranteed and contingent interests. What problems arise?

Notes

E. FISCHER & P. SWISHER, Principles of Insurance Law, Introduction to Property Insurance, p. 103; What Constitutes an Insurable Interest, p. 103 (Matthew Bender, 1986); R. HENDERSON, Insurance Law, *LaCras v. Hughes*, p. 21; *Lucena v. Craufurd*, p. 22; *Brewton v. Alabama Farm Bureau Mut. Cas. Ins. Co.*, p. 25; notes, pp. 26-28 (Michie, 1989); R. JERRY, Understanding Insurance Law, §42 (Matthew Bender, 1987); R. KEETON & A. WIDISS, Insurance Law, §3.4(a)(5) (West, 1988); R. KEETON, Basic Insurance Law, *National Filtering Oil Co. v. Citizens' Ins. Co.*, p. 141; *Farmers Mutual Ins. Co. v. New Holland Turnpike Co.*, p. 144 (West, 1977); A. WIDISS, Insurance, The Principle of Indemnity, p. 123; The Insurable Interest Doctrine, p. 123; History, p. 124 (West, 1989); K. YORK & J. WHELAN, Insurance Law (Second Edition), Pinzur, Insurable Interest: A Search for Consistency, p. 192 (West, 1988); W. YOUNG & E. HOLMES, Insurance, The Insurable Interest Requirement, p. 124; Varieties of Insurable Interests, p. 426; notes, pp. 427-28 (Foundation, 1985).

Problem 47

Bob and Mary Jane Russell agreed to purchase a single family home being sold by Albert and Anna Gilbert. Bob and Mary Jane had fallen in love with the home when first shown it by their Realtor, Pat Skelly. The contract provided, among other things, for the following:

1. Downpayment of 10% of the $100,000 purchase price. This money was provided by Bob's parents, who loaned the young couple the full $10,000 on the condition that they use it as part of the purchase price of the

house;

2. Approval of an $80,000 mortgage by Second National Bank, at current rates;

3. Access to the house by Wilson Construction Co., which was hired by Bob and Mary Jane to replace the roof, add skylights in two rooms and add a back porch, at a cost of $15,000, of which $5,000 had been paid as a downpayment. The contract also contained provisions which indicated that if the buyers could not obtain mortgage financing, these improvements would be paid for by the sellers, who had previously contemplated this work;

4. A commission of 7% of the $100,000 selling price to Pat Skelly, to be paid by the seller.

The day after the contract was signed by all parties and the downpayment paid into the escrow account of Pat Skelly, Bob and Mary Jane applied for their mortgage at Second National Bank. The officer who took their application told them it would take about 15 days for the bank to act upon the loan application. The next day, Wilson Construction Co. began work on the house. On the fourth, and last day of their work, a Wilson employee negligently dropped a cigarette onto a rag which a fellow employee had coated with gasoline to wipe paint spills. The resulting fire caused extensive damage to the Wilson improvements and the house.

Questions

1. On the day after the contracts were signed, Albert and Anna Gilbert purchased a 60 day extension of their insurance on the home, which

insurance was expiring. Additionally, Bob and Mary Jane Russell, Bob's parents, the Wilson Construction Co., and Pat Skelly each purchased insurance on the property. Which of them had an insurable interest?

2. Assume that the contract to purchase by Bob and Mary Jane was an oral contract. After the fire, the various insurance companies all seek to defeat the claims on the basis that the contract violated the statute of frauds. What result?

3. Assume that the various insurance companies seek to defeat insurable interest on the basis that the contract is contingent on approval of the loan. Will this be successful?

4. On the day Bob and Mary Jane Russell applied for their loan, and pursuant to Second National's standard practice, Forrest Gray, the loan officer who took the Russell loan application, immediately sought to purchase insurance on the property. Should he be successful?

5. Assume that Gray was successful in obtaining the insurance. The bank acted with unaccustomed speed and approved the loan in two days. Thus, the loan was approved the day before the fire. After the fire, the bank's insurance company seeks to defend on the basis that Second National had no insurable interest when they purchased the insurance.

Problem 48

Sometime after purchasing their new home, Bob and Mary Jane Russell began experiencing financial reversals due to a significant downturn in both of their businesses. As a result, several months went by with the Russells making no payment on their home mortgage with Second National Bank. Additionally, Bob and Mary Jane had made no payment on a $10,000 loan from Bob's parents which was made with the understanding that the money would be used as part of the downpayment on the home. Additionally, no property taxes were paid on the home.

Following the original closing, Bob and Mary Jane Russell, Second National Bank, and Bob's parents all purchased insurance policies on the property.

Questions

1. Assume that after foreclosure proceedings were begun by Second National, the home burns. Are any of the policies defeated by a claim of no insurable interest?

2. Assume that after receiving notice of impending foreclosure, Bob and Mary Jane decided to deed the property over to Second National, in satisfaction of the mortgage. They remain liable on the debt to Bob's parents. Fire damages the home. Are any of the policies defeated by a claim of no insurable interest?

3. Assume that foreclosure proceedings are begun, and that a court decree has been entered in favor of Second National granting foreclosure to Second National Bank and ordering a sale of the property. At this time the home burns. Are any of the policies defeated by a claim of no insurable interest?

4. Assume that a foreclosure sale was held yesterday and that Randall Sinclair, a third-party real estate tycoon, purchased the property at the sale. The house burned last night. Are any of the policies defeated by a claim of no insurable interest? Suppose Second National, after Sinclair made a low bid at the sale, bid the amount of its judgment and purchased the house. Does your answer change?

5. Assume, instead, that before a foreclosure proceeding could be started by Second National, the Collector of Revenue for the City in which the house was located, began a foreclosure proceeding for the past due taxes. The proceeding was commenced, a sale was held, and Randall Sinclair, a third-party real estate tycoon, purchased the property at the sale. Under the law, however, a further court proceeding is needed to determine if the sale price to the third party was fair. While this proceeding was pending, the house burns. Are any of the policies defeated by a claim of no insurable interest?

6. In any of these cases, if the insurance company seeks to deny coverage on the basis of absence of insurable interest, must the company take any affirmative actions?

7. Who will have the burden of proof on the issue of insurable interest?

Notes

E. FISCHER & P. SWISHER, Principles of Insurance Law, *Castle Cars, Inc. v. United States Fire Ins. Co.*, p. 105; *Isabell v. Aetna Ins. Co.*, p. 108; questions and notes, pp. 110-11; Patterson, Essentials of Insurance Law, p. 111; *Kingston v. Great Southwest Fire Ins. Co.*, p. 113; *Tublitz v. Glens Falls Ins. Co.*, p. 116; *Chicago Title & Trust Co. v. United States Fidelity & Guaranty Co.*, p. 118; Waiver of Estoppel Introduction, p. 119; *Allstate Ins. Co. v. Moore*, p. 120; notes & questions, p. 123 (Matthew Bender, 1986); R. HENDERSON, Insurance Law, *LaCras v. Hughes*, p. 21; *Lucena v. Craufurd*, p. 22; *Brewton v. Alabama Farm Bureau Mut. Cas. Ins. Co.*, p. 25; notes, pp. 26-28; *Sun Ins. Office of London v. Merz*, p. 38; *Dalby v. The India & London Life Ass. Co.*, p. 39, notes, pp. 43-45 (Michie, 1989); R. JERRY, Understanding

Insurance Law, §§42; 43; 44; 46[c] (Matthew Bender, 1987); R. KEETON & A. WIDISS, Insurance Law, §§3.1-3.4 (West, 1988); R. KEETON, Basic Insurance Law, *Insurance Co. v. Stinson*, p. 124; *Hartford Fire Ins. Co. v. Cagle*, p. 127; *Cherokee Foundries, Inc. v. Imperial Assurance Co.*, p. 128; *LeCras v. Hughes*, p. 136; *Lucena v. Craufurd*, p. 137; *National Filtering Oil Co. v. Citizens' Ins. Co.*, p. 141; *Farmers Mutual Ins. Co. v. New Holland Turnpike Co.*, p. 144; *Van Cure v. Hartford Fire Ins. Co.*, p. 148; statutes, pp. 155-59; *Colver v. Central States Fire Ins. Co.*, p. 160; *Liverpool & London & Globe Ins. Co. v. Bolling*, p. 161; *Macaura v. Northern Assurance Co., Ltd.*, p. 168 (West, 1977); A. WIDISS, Insurance, The Right to Question Insurable Interest, p. 139; *Insurance Company v. Stinson*, p. 140; *Jason's Foods, Inc. v. Peter Eckrich & Sons, Inc.*, p. 143 (West, 1989); K. YORK & J. WHELAN, Insurance Law (Second Edition), Pinzur, Insurable Interest: A Search for Consistency, p. 192; *Tublitz v. Glen Falls Ins. Co.*, p. 198; note 1, pp. 199-200; *Miller v. New Jersey Ins. Underwriters Ass'n.*, p. 201; *Christ Gospel Temple v. Liberty Mutual Ins. Co.*, p. 205 (West, 1988); W. YOUNG & E. HOLMES, Insurance, Contractual Rights & Insurable Interest, p. 428; *Village of Constantine v. Home Ins. Co.*, p. 429, notes, pp. 432-33; statutes, pp. 433-34; notes, p. 434; *Boston Insurance Co. v. Beckett*, p. 434; notes, pp. 434-35; Limited Interests, p. 436; notes, pp. 438-39 (Foundation, 1985).

PROBLEM 49

Albert Morrissey testified that he purchased a five year old luxury automobile from a Mr. Marr for $3,000. Morrissey insured the vehicle with Car Insurance. Subsequently, the car was damaged in an automobile accident caused by Morrissey and in which Marilyn Johnny, the driver of the other involved vehicle was seriously injured. Ms. Grinch, Car Insurer's claims adjuster, testified that her investigation had shown the vehicle in question to have been stolen prior to its purchase by Morrissey. Further, Car Insurance adduced evidence to the effect that the average retail on a vehicle of this type at the time of the purported sale to Morrissey was $7,000, and that Mr. Morrissey had failed to register the vehicle.

Questions

1. Does Morrissey have the kind of "factual expectancy" interest in the car which would normally support a finding of "insurable interest?"

2. Will Morrissey collect for the damage to the car? Why or why not?

3. Should Marilyn Johnny be able to collect for her personal injuries? Why or why not?

Problem 50

Ricky purchased a classic sports car from a Mr. Douglas who provided Ricky with a title describing a car of that model. The title contained the vehicle identification number (VIN) 1567932M745902. Ricky looked for the VIN on the car, but was unable to find it. Nevertheless, Ricky sent in the title to the Department of Revenue and received in return a new title to the vehicle in his name. Ricky insured the vehicle with Fast Insurance. One month later Ricky's car was stolen. In the course of the police investigation which followed, it was discovered that Ricky's car previously had been stolen from a Mr. Fats. The Fats car VIN was 178956P008714. The police found out that the title and VIN 1567932M745902 that Ricky had received from Mr. Douglas belonged to a wrecked vehicle of the same model and year as the Fats automobile. Fast Insurance contends that Ricky had no insurable interest in the car which he purported to register and insure because of his failure to comply with a state registration and licensing statute which provides:

> It shall be unlawful for any person to buy or sell in this state any motor vehicle or trailer registered under the laws of this state, unless, at the time of the delivery thereof, there shall pass between the parties such certificates of ownership with an assignment thereof, as herein provided, and the sale of any

> motor vehicle or trailer registered under the laws of this state, without the assignment of such certificate of ownership, shall be fraudulent and void.

Fast Insurance argues that, in the absence of such compliance, Ricky failed to become the owner of the vehicle and therefore had no insurable interest in it. Ricky argues that the only issue is whether he was a good faith purchaser for value. What result? Why?

Notes

E. FISCHER & P. SWISHER, Principles of Insurance Law, ***Castle Cars, Inc. v. United States Fire Ins. Co.***, p. 105; notes & questions, p. 108 (Matthew Bender, 1986); R. JERRY, Understanding Insurance Law, §46[b] (Matthew Bender, 1987); R. KEETON & A. WIDISS, Insurance Law, §3.4(a)(5) at 162-64 (West, 1988); R. KEETON, Basic Insurance Law, *Scarola v. Insurance Co. of North America*, p. 164 (West, 1977); A. WIDISS, Insurance, *Pennsylvania National Mutual Casualty Ins. Co. v. State Farm Mutual Auto. Ins. Co.*, p. 134; *American Mutual Fire Ins. Co. v. Passmore*, p. 137 (West, 1989); K. YORK & J. WHELAN, Insurance Law (Second Edition), note 2, pp. 200-201 (West, 1988); W. YOUNG & E. HOLMES, Insurance, Note 4, pp. 435-36 (Foundation, 1985).

B. Warranties, Representations, Concealment

Problem 51

When he applied for insurance on property he had recently purchased, Larry Lagman filled out an application for insurance with Heritage Casualty Company. Assume that the insurance applied for issued, and that thereafter a fire destroyed a portion of the property.

Questions

1. In the application, Larry was asked the question: "Are premises to be occupied during the entire term of this policy?" While Larry knew they were not yet occupied, he intended to rent the building as soon as he could. He thus answered "Yes." In signing the application, Larry read and understood the following statement: "Applicant WARRANTS that all of the foregoing statements are true and accurate. Applicant understands that if any such statement is false, any policy which issues on the basis of this application shall be void." Although Larry never saw the application again, the policy issued. In fact, due to a downturn in the economy, Larry was unable to attract tenants and the property remained vacant for 8 months before the fire and was vacant at the time of the fire. Heritage refuses to pay based upon breach of warranty. What result? Who bears the ultimate risk of non-persuasion?

2. Assume that in the preceding question, the application, with the same statements, was attached to the policy. Again, Heritage refuses payment. What result? Who bears the risk of non-persuasion?

3. Assume that the foregoing questions were not asked, but that Larry was asked: "Are all property taxes paid?" In fact they were not paid, and Larry knew it, yet he answered "Yes." When he received the insurance policy, which had the application attached, Larry read the following statement: "It is understood and agreed that the insurance herein is expressly conditioned upon the truthfulness of all statements contained in the application for insurance, if that application is attached." Following the fire, Heritage refuses to pay based on the false statement about property tax. What result? Who bears the risk

of non-persuasion?

4. Assume that the foregoing questions were not asked, but that Larry was asked in the application: "Has applicant ever made a claim on any fire insurance policy whatsoever?" Despite the fact that he had three fire losses on previously owned property, Larry answered "No." The application called for his signature which he added. The application was attached to the policy which issued. After the fire, Heritage refuses payment. What result? Who bears the risk of non-persuasion.

5. Assume that in the preceding question, the application was not attached to the policy which issued. How do your answers change?

6. Assume that Larry deliberately lied about the prior fire claims, but that each of the claims was made to Heritage Casualty Co. and was listed in the Company computer under Larry's name. Do your answers change? How?

7. Assume that when Larry was asked about prior fire claims, Larry told the agent to whom the application was given: "Well, you know about the three claims that I made on my truck." And the agent said, "Yes, we know, but this is insurance for property and is not the same," and, as a result, Larry wrote "No." In fact, all three of his fire claims had been on a truck which he had owned. Heritage refuses to pay for the loss to the real estate. What result? Who bears the risk of non-persuasion?

8. As to each of these questions, how will you plead the case on Larry's behalf? How do you expect Heritage to respond? By Answer? By Answer and Defenses? By Counterclaim? How or will you respond to Heritage's pleading?

Problem 52

Dave Roberts was fond of motorcycles. For years, he collected parts from various Harley-Davidson motorcycles that he found around his town. In 1981, he assembled all of the parts into his own 1200 cc Harley. When he went to register the motorcycle with the Division of Motor Vehicles, Dave was asked for the year of the motorcycle. Dave figured that since he made it in 1981, that was the year of manufacture and gave that year. He received a title certificate for the motorcycle and took that to his local insurance agent to obtain insurance coverage. Dave told the agent that he wanted insurance for his "new 1981 Harley" and gave the agent the title certificate. If Dave had informed the agent of the fact that the motorcycle was made of various parts of other motorcycles, the Company would have had to consider the ability of the company to make a determination of value of the various parts used to construct the motorcycle. Dave's application was attached to his insurance policy. After the motorcycle was involved in a crash, Insurance Company refused to make payment, claiming that Dave had concealed the true facts from it. Dave will testify that he honestly believed that he had a 1981 Harley, and that he was not trying to deceive anyone. In fact, Insurance Company cannot now decide whether it would have written the policy or not.

Questions

1. Assume that Insurance Company claims concealment? What result?

Who bears the risk of non-persuasion?

2. What is the effect of Dave's claim that he did not intend to deceive anyone?

3. What is the import of testimony by Insurance Company representatives that they do not know if they would have written the policy, even if they had known of the facts?

PROBLEM 53

In her application for insurance on her new Condominium, Andrea Stout was asked the question: "Has applicant ever had any other property insurance cancelled or rated up by any company?" Despite the fact that her recent tenant policy was cancelled after she had made 7 claims in 3 years, and refused to give a sworn proof of loss on her 8th claim, Andrea answered "No." The application, signed by Andrea, was attached to the policy which issued. After a fire in the condominium, the company learned of Andrea's prior insurance cancellation and refused to pay, although it did return the premium to her. Andrea has now sued for her damage and demanded a jury trial. The Company is resisting the issue of jury trial claiming that the issues to be tried are ones of law. Discuss.

Notes

E. FISCHER & P. SWISHER, Principles of Insurance Law, §§3.01--3.03 at pp. 165-279 (Matthew Bender, 1986); R. HENDERSON, Insurance Law, Warranties & Conditions, p. 345; *Omaha Sky Divers*

Parachute Club, Inc. v. Ranger Ins. Co., p. 348; note, pp. 350-51; *Allstate Ins. Co. v. Boggs*, p. 853; notes, pp. 855-56; *Charles, Henry & Crowley, Co. v. Home Ins. Co.*, p. 856; *Howard v. Federal Crop Ins. Corp.*, p. 858; notes, p. 862; statutes, pp. 862-864; notes, pp. 864-65; *O'Connor v. Proprietors Ins. Co.*, p. 865; notes, pp. 871-72 (Michie, 1989); R. JERRY, Understanding Insurance Law, §§62B; 100--104A (Matthew Bender, 1987); R. KEETON & A. WIDISS, Insurance Law, §§5.6-5.8 (West, 1988); R. KEETON, Basic Insurance Law, Notes, pp. 530-31; Concepts of Warranty in Insurance Law, pp. 628-630; statutes, pp. 634-644; *Moe v. Allemannia Fire Ins. Co.*, p. 644; *Omaha Sky Divers Parachute Club, Inc. v. Ranger Ins. Co.*, p. 646; *Mc Pherson v. Camden Fire Ins. Co.*, p. 654; *Security State Bank v. Aetna Ins. Co.*, p. 654; *Employers' Liability Assurance Corp. v. Vella*, p. 656 (West, 1977); A. WIDISS, Insurance, §§5.6--5.8 (West, 1989); K. YORK & J. WHELAN, Insurance Law (Second Edition), *Knight v. United States Fire Ins. Co.*, p. 96; statutes, pp. 100-103; notes on Concealment, pp. 106-107; introductory note, pp. 242-44; *Campbell v. Hartford Fire Ins. Co.*, p. 244; *Reid v. Hardware Mutual Ins. Co. of the Carolinas*, p. 246; *Vlastos v. Sumitomo Marine & Fire Ins. Co.*, p. 248; *American Home Assurance Co. v. Harvey's Wagon Wheel, Inc.*, p. 252; *Los Angeles Mutual Ins. Co. v. Cawog*, p. 253; statutes, pp. 257-59; note, pp. 259-260; An Exercise in Analysis, pp. 260-63 (West, 1988); W. YOUNG & E. HOLMES, Insurance, Chapter 3 A--E at pp. 141--226 (Foundation, 1985).

C. Absence of Coverage (Exclusions, Implied and Express; No Coverage)

1. Generally

Problem 54

Daniel Charles had his home insured against fire by a policy which contained the provisions of the New York Standard Fire Insurance Policy, as mandated by state administrative regulation. Because of a recent severe drought, the City Council of Charles' home enacted an Ordinance which banned all outdoor burning, including the use of any charcoal or exterior gas grills. The Ordinance provided for a fine of $50 upon the first conviction under the Ordinance and $100 plus 10 days in jail for subsequent convictions.

Charles, unaware of the Ordinance, lighted his charcoal barbecue grill on his back porch, the coals set fire to a parched nearby bush, which in turn ignited Charles' home. Charles was summoned, convicted, and fined $50 plus all court costs as a first offender under the Municipal Ordinance. Following the fire and Charles conviction under the Ordinance, the Insurance Company refused payment to Charles for the damage to his home. If Charles now files suit to collect, who should win?

Problem 55

Daniel Charles had his home insured against fire by a policy which copied from the New York Standard Fire Insurance Policy, as mandated by state administrative regulation. Following the freezing of his water pipes last winter, Charles went into his basement, with his new blowtorch and tried to heat the pipes to thaw them out. His success was mixed in that, while the pipes did warm, they warmed so much as to ignite the entire house, causing extensive damage. The Insurance Company which issued the fire policy refuses coverage. If Charles files suit to collect, who will win?

Notes

R. KEETON & A. WIDISS, Insurance Law, §6.6(c)(2) (West, 1988); R. KEETON, Basic Insurance Law, *Todd v. Traders' & Mechanics' Ins. Co.*, p. 439; *Goldman v. Piedmont Fire Ins. Co.*, p. 666; notes, pp. 677-78 (West, 1977); K. YORK & J. WHELAN, Insurance Law (Second Edition), Problem 2, pp. 273-74 (West, 1988).

2. Friendly Fires

Problem 56

Spurred by a spirit of energy conservation, Sallie and Ron Channel included a wood burning stove/heater in their new home which served to both cook some of their meals and provide substantial heat to their home. One afternoon, Sallie decided to light a fire so the home would be warm for the evening. Soon, Sallie noticed smoke in the house; which was soon replaced by flame. Investigation revealed that accumulated soot in the chimney caught fire and caused the damage. Sallie and Ron had fire insurance with First Security Insurance Co., which has denied coverage. Is this correct? Why?

Notes

E. FISCHER & P. SWISHER, Principles of Insurance Law, *Schulze & Burch Biscuit Co. v. American Protection Ins. Co.*, p. 333; notes & questions, pp. 333-34 (Matthew Bender, 1986); R. HENDERSON, Insurance Law, *Youse v. Employers' Fire Ins. Co.*, p. 142; *Engel v. Redwood County Farmers Mut. Ins. Co.*, p. 146 (Michie, 1989); R. JERRY, Understanding Insurance Law, §66 (Matthew Bender, 1987); R. KEETON & A. WIDISS, Insurance Law, §5.3(d) (West, 1988); R. KEETON, Basic Insurance Law, *Youse v. Employers Fire Ins. Co.*, p. 434 (West, 1977); A. WIDISS, Insurance, *Schulze & Burch Biscuit v. A.M. Protection Ins.*, p. 438 (West, 1989); K. YORK & J. WHELAN, Insurance Law (Second Edition), *Engel v. Redwood County Farmers Mutual Ins. Co.*, p. 237; questions, p. 240 (West, 1988); W. YOUNG & E. HOLMES, Insurance, *Barcalo Manufacturing Co. v. Firemen's Mut. Ins. Co.*, p. 511; notes, pp. 514-15 (Foundation, 1985).

3. Intentional Acts

Problem 57

Fox, Maris, Morgan, Cobb, and Baker were all partners in Racquets, an indoor racquetball club. Baker was the "general" partner in that he owned 50% of the outstanding shares, while the other 4 were all limited partners, owning approximately 12% each. After several years of severe financial losses, Baker either set fire to the club, or had the fire set. Baker was killed in the fire. Charter General Insurance, which held the fire insurance on the property, has refused payment to the remaining partners because of the intentional act of the general partner. What result? Why?

PROBLEM 58

Bonnie and Ben Valle, brother and sister, were the owners of Bennie's Bar-B-Q, which was insured for fire by Atlantic Property and Casualty Insurance Co. After several years of financial losses, Ben Valle owed utility bills on the restaurant and on his home; owed back property taxes on his home and owed back sales tax on the business; was behind in his home mortgage; and had checks returned for non-sufficient funds on both his personal and business checking accounts. As investigators later concluded, Ben Valle had substantial motivation for arson. The Bar-B-Q was substantially damaged by a fire which occurred in the wee hours of the morning. Ben Valle had no alibi for the period in which the fire took place--and several early morning joggers saw a man matching Valle's description on the roof of the Bar-B-Q at about the time the smoke began to billow from the building. The fire department labeled the fire as "probable arson." After the fire, Ben Valle completed a

"Proof of Loss" for $92,000 to Atlantic Property and Casualty Company in which he stated as the cause of loss: "fire in a Bar-B-Q oven causing overheating which eventually escaped." Atlantic Property refused payment of the loss on two grounds:

1. The fire was started by arson by a named insured;
2. The named insured filed a fraudulent proof of loss.

You represent Bonnie Valle, who did not actively participate in the operation of the Bar-B-Q, but who contributed money. Bonnie was not even in town at the time of the fire, and there is no claim that she was in any way responsible for the loss. She is a named insured on the Atlantic Property Policy and she had reviewed the Proof of Loss before it was filed, but saw nothing unusual about it. Can she collect on the policy?

Notes

R. HENDERSON, Insurance Law, *Kulubis v. Texas Farm Bureau Underwriters Ins. Co.*, p. 436; note, p. 438 (Michie, 1989); R. JERRY, Understanding Insurance Law, §63A (Matthew Bender, 1987); R. KEETON & A. WIDISS, Insurance Law, §§5.4(c)(4), 7.2(f) (West, 1988); R. KEETON, Basic Insurance Law, *Todd v. Traders' and Mechanics' Ins. Co.*, p. 439; (West, 1977); A. WIDISS, Insurance, *Bryan v. Employers National Ins. Co.*, p. 413 (West, 1989); K. YORK & J. WHELAN, Insurance Law (Second Edition), Notes, p. 241 (West, 1988).

4. Coverage Questions Versus Exclusions

Problem 59

Melba Johnson sustained damage to her home and its contents in a fire last spring. Melba had an insurance policy with North State Insurance Company which provided for loss from fire 1.) for damage to Johnson's house; 2.) for damage to the contents; and 3.) for living expenses. The policy also provided: "This entire policy shall be void if *** after a loss, the insured has willfully concealed or misrepresented any material fact or circumstance concerning this insurance or the subject thereof ***." Johnson admittedly submitted a materially false schedule of personal property allegedly lost in the fire. North State has contended that this false claim entitles it to deny coverage for the damage to the home and the lost living expenses as well. What result? Who bears the ultimate risk of nonpersuasion?

Problem 60

Jim McCulley had his 3 year old thirty-ton capacity dump truck insured by Land and Sea Insurance Co. under a policy which provided for recovery of damage to the truck caused by a "Collision:"

> "Collision" means that your vehicle upset or hit or was hit by a vehicle or other object.
>
> There is no coverage for loss to any vehicle due to wear and tear, freezing, mechanical breakdown or failure.

Shortly after he purchased the truck, McCulley had driven it over a ditch and had caused a small crack in the frame. That damage was repaired by welding "fish plates" on both sides of the frame. While covered by this policy, McCulley loaded the truck with about 10 tons of gravel. Noticing that the load was not evenly distributed, McCulley tried to move the dump truck and in doing so struck a metal post. The tailgate, which attaches to the frame of the truck was damaged. McCulley then completed the move he was trying to make, stopped the truck and loaded a small additional amount of gravel into the truck. It was at that point that the frame on the truck collapsed. Land and Sea refuses to pay for the damage claiming that the damage was caused by a breakdown and not by a collision. What result? Who bears the ultimate risk of non-persuasion?

Problem 61

Katherine Stuffle owned her own home and was insured by House and Land Insurance Co. Her policy provided, in part:

> This policy insures for direct loss to property caused by *** windstorm or hail.
>
> This policy does not include loss to the interior of the subject property caused by rain unless the direct force of wind or hail damages the building causing an opening in a roof or wall and the rain enters through this opening.

A terrible wind tore a gutter off of the roof of Stuffle's home causing the gutter to hang down in a point over the porch. The wind was blowing toward the house on that side. Water running out of the gutter accumulated to about 6 inches on the porch and eventually ran into the basement causing damage. There were no cracks in the basement wall or siding. House and Land refuses payment. What result? Who bears the risk of non-persuasion?

Problem 62

Rubber garments valued at $10m recently purchased for Big Q Imports were stored at the premises of Robyn Storage. Robyn had insured its premises and contents for $2m with Hayes Insurance, having estimated the total value of the premises at $1m. That policy provided in relevant part:

> Provided the insured is legally liable therefor, this policy also shall cover merchandise held in trust or on commission, or sold but not delivered ***. In consideration of the reduced rates under which this policy is written, coverage is expressly conditioned that in the event of loss this Company shall be liable for no greater proportion thereof than the amount hereby assured bears to Seventy-Five Per Cent (75%) of the value of the property described herein.

A fire destroyed Robyn's premises, the Big Q goods and other property owned by Robyn valued at $1m.

In denying Robyn's claim of $12m, Hayes Insurance has made the following arguments:

(i) The policy did not insure Big Q's property but only Robyn's potential legal liability to Big Q. Hayes had no responsibility under the policy until notified under the terms of the policy of a legal claim made by Big Q.

(ii) In no event should any coverage by Hayes exceed $3m.

Questions

1. You represent Robyn. What are your best arguments?

2. Should any proceeds of the insurance be paid to the bailor or the bailee?

Notes

E. FISCHER & P. SWISHER, Principles of Insurance Law, *Marshall Produce Co. v. St. Paul Fire & Marine Ins. Co.*, p. 326; notes & questions, pp. 330-31; *Northwest Airlines, Inc. v. Globe Indemnity Co.*, p. 340; notes & questions, p. 345; *Graham v. Public Employees Mut. Ins. Co.*, p. 352; notes & questions, pp. 356-57; *Bohnen International v. Liberty Mut. Ins. Co.*, p. 361; *United States Automobile Ass'n. v. Park*, p. 364; notes & questions, pp. 365-66; *Continental Cas. Co. v. Gilbane Building Co.*, p. 367; *Qualls v. Country Mut. Ins. Co.*, p. 371; notes & questions, pp. 372-73; *Vargas v. Ins. Co. of North America*, p. 373; notes & questions, pp. 376-77; *Compagnie Des Bauxites v. Insurance Co. of North America*, p. 436; notes & questions, pp. 439-440 (Matthew Bender, 1986); R. HENDERSON, Insurance Law, *Compagnie Des Bauxites v. Insurance Co. of North America*, p. 133; *Texas Eastern Transmission v. Marine Office--Appleton & Cox, Corp.*, p. 137; notes, pp. 141-42; *Chute v. North River Ins. Co.*, p. 170; *Terrien v. Pawtucket Mut. Fire Ins. Co.*, p. 172; *Omaha Paper Stock Co. v. Harbor Ins. Co.*, p. 234; notes, pp. 241-44 (Michie, 1989); R. JERRY, Understanding Insurance Law, §62B (Matthew Bender, 1987); R. KEETON & A. WIDISS, Insurance Law, §§4.5, 4.6, 5.5(c), 6.6(b) (West, 1988); R. KEETON, Basic Insurance Law, *United States v. Globe & Rutgers Fire Ins. Co.*, p. 324; *Globe & Rutgers Fire Ins. Co. v. United States*, p. 328; *Texas City Terminal Railway Co. v. American Equitable Assurance Co.*, p. 329; *Bruener v. Twin City Fire Ins. Co.*, p. 503; *Ploe v. International Indemnity Co.*, p. 506; *Harris v. Allstate Ins. Co.*, p. 506; *Mammina v. Homeland Ins. Co.*, p. 508; *Boston Camping Distributor Co. v. Lumbermens Mutual Casualty Co.*, p. 522; *Fawcett House, Inc. v. Great Cent. Ins. Co.*, p. 524; *Providence Washington Ins. Co. v. Proffitt*, p. 526; *United States Ins. Co. v. Boyer*, p. 529; *Farmers Ins. Exchange v. Wallace*, p. 529 (West, 1977); A. WIDISS, Insurance, *Jason's Foods, Inc. v. Peter Eckrich & Sons, Inc.*, p. 143; Introductory Note, p. 265; Identifying Insureds, p. 266; Interests in Personal Property Held, p. 313; Introductory Note, p. 406; Approaches to Defining the Risks Transferred, p. 407; *Zimmer v. Aetna Ins. Co., p. 506;* Graham v. Public Employees Mut. Ins. Co..(, p. 509; *O'Connor v. Proprietors Ins. Co.*, p. 513 (West, 1989); K. YORK & J. WHELAN, Insurance Law (Second Edition), *Cochran v. MFA Mutual Ins. Co.*, p. 209; notes, p. 211; Note, How Coverage is Defined in Property Insurance, pp. 211-214; *Bird v. St. Paul Fire & Marine Ins. Co.*, p. 215; *Pan-American World Airlines, Inc. v. Aetna Casualty & Surety Corp.*, p. 218; *Graham v. Public Employees Mutual Ins. Co.*, p. 220; note, pp. 224-25; An Exercise in Analysis, pp. 226-27 (West, 1988); W. YOUNG & E. HOLMES, Insurance, *Goodman v. Fireman's Fund Ins. Co.*, p. 515; notes, pp. 516-18; *Island Rivers Service Corp. v. Hartford Fire Ins. Co.*, p. 518 (Foundation, 1985).

D. Measure of Recovery

Problem 63

Mary Daniels' 1957 Ford Thunderbird was destroyed when it was struck by a semi-trailer while stopped at a traffic light near Mary's home. Mary has an automobile insurance policy which covers her automobile when it is struck by another vehicle and which will pay the "Actual Cash Value of the damaged property." Mary received the car three years ago following the death of her mother, the original owner. Mary has always kept the car garaged, but she has used it as her principal car. It has 96,000 miles, and has received regular servicing. Mary recalls that her mother purchased the car new for about $2,900. She has checked in her lending library and can find no current NADA Used Car price for the car and she has been advised by her local Ford dealer that there is no "bluebook" value calculated for cars that old. In last Sunday's newspaper, she saw two advertised--one listed a "'57 T-Bird, usable for parts only--$1100 or best offer." Another listed "Mint '57 Thunderbird; formerly owned by collector and used for shows only, $13,000." Mary really does not like the car; thinking that it is too small for her use; as a result, she recently told a friend--"If someone would offer me $5000 for this thing, I'd take it gladly."

Questions

1. How much should Mary receive?

2. Who will testify as to the actual cash value of the vehicle?

3. Are there other factors which the court could consider in determining the actual cash value? What?

Problem 64

Several years ago, Ralph Anthony purchased a small house and lot for $50,000. Ralph was not the best housekeeper in the world, so he allowed the interior of the property to fall into disarray. Additionally, he did very little to maintain the exterior of the house or the land. Because of the closing of his town's largest employer, many homes in Ralph's town recently went up for sale, further driving down an already depressed housing market. When Ralph purchased the house, he contacted his local insurance agent and purchased $100,000 worth of fire insurance on the property. The insurance agent made no investigation and did not attempt to lower the amount of coverage, which has remained on the house ever since. Last week, the house burned, leaving only the chimney standing. It would cost approximately $52,000 to replace the house. The Insurance Company has insisted on payment of that amount, which a court would consider fair and reasonable under the existing real estate market conditions.

Questions

1. Are there any legislative provisions which would compel payment to Ralph of more money?

2. What is the purpose of any such provisions?

3. Assume the house had recently been condemned, and, although Ralph had not signed the deed over to the condemning authority, he had received a check from the condemning authority for $52,000, the amount ordered by the Court as compensation.

Problem 65

Michael and Edith Grant purchased their home in the University Park subdivision 30 years ago when Michael was first employed as a University Professor. The home was made of some excellent locally-made brick and was constructed by one carpenter/mason who had an excellent reputation. Michael and Edith paid $39,900 for the 4 bedroom, 2 bath home. They raised 3 children in the house and watched their neighborhood grow from younger couples to older soon-to-be-retireds. The home grew old as well. Michael and Edith always maintained fire insurance on their home with Good Hands Insurance Company. When their house was recently revalued because of statewide property reassessment, the home was valued at $125,000 and Michael and Edith have insurance for that amount. In a discussion with a builder friend recently, however, Michael was told: "Anytime you want to sell me your house for $125,000, let me know. You could hardly replace the wood for that today; let alone try to rebuild the place." Michael and Edith love their home, want to continue to live in it and would want it replaced if lost. They have always assumed that if a fire destroyed the home, the insurance would pay to construct one like it. What advice can you give?

Notes

E. FISCHER & P. SWISHER, Principles of Insurance Law, *Ohio Casualty Ins. Co. v. Ramsey*, p. 538; notes & questions, pp. 543-45; *Magrath v. Mechanics & Traders Ins. Co.*, p. 545; notes & questions, p. 548; *Higgins v. Hanover Ins. Co.*, p. 549; notes & questions, pp. 552-53; *Safeco Ins. Co. of America v. Sharma*, p. 553; notes & questions, pp. 556-57; *Paramount Fire Ins. Co. v. Aetna Cas. & Surety Co.*, p. 559;

notes & questions, pp. 561-62 (Matthew Bender, 1986); R. HENDERSON, Insurance Law, *Elberon Bathing Co. v. Ambassador Ins. Co.*, p. 49; *Doelger & Kirsten, Inc. v. National Union Fire Ins. Co.*, p. 54; *Bailey v. Gulf Ins. Co.*, p. 55; notes, pp. 57-58; *Higgins v. Insurance Co. of North America*, p. 58; *Crisp v. Security National Ins. Co.*, p. 62; *Mieske v. Bartell Drug Co.*, p. 65; notes, p. 67; *Aetna Cas. & Surety Co. v. Insurance Dep't. of Iowa*, p. 67; notes, p. 69; *Heady v. Farmers Mut. Ins. Co.*, p. 81; notes, pp. 84-85 (Michie, 1989); R. JERRY, Understanding Insurance Law, §§93[a], [c], [d], [e] (Matthew Bender, 1987); R. KEETON & A. WIDISS, Insurance Law, §§3.9, 3.12(a) (West, 1988); R. KEETON, Basic Insurance Law, Excerpts, pp. 192-202; *Jefferson Ins. Co. of N.Y. v. Superior Court*, p. 202; *Bailey v. Gulf Ins. Co*, p. 207; *Doelger & Kirsten, Inc. v. National Union Fire Ins. Co.*, p. 209; *McAnarney v. Newark Fire Ins. Co.*, p. 213, Excerpts, pp. 206-207 (West, 1977); A. WIDISS, Insurance, Introductory Note, p. 183; *Elberon Bathing Co. v. Ambassador Ins. Co.*, p. 186; *Travelers Indemnity v. Armstrong*, p. 191; *National Fire Ins. Co. of Hartford v. Solomon*, p. 198; Obsolescence, p. 204; *Garcy Corp. v. Home Ins. Co.*, p. 206; Valued Policies in Real Property Insurance, p. 250; *Heady v. Farmers Mut. Ins. Co.*, p. 251; *Stahlberg v. Travelers Indemnity Co.*, p. 257 (West, 1989); K. YORK & J. WHELAN, Insurance Law (Second Edition), *Titus v. West American Ins. Co.*, p. 288; *McAnarney v. Newark Fire Ins. Co.*, p. 294; notes, pp. 297-98 (West, 1988); W. YOUNG & E. HOLMES, Insurance, Measure of Insurer's Liability, p. 488; *Elberon Bathing v. Ambassador Ins. Co.*, p. 489; notes, pp. 499-501; Adjusting Partial Building Losses, p. 501; notes, p. 502; Valued Policies, p. 502; notes, pp. 503-504; Valued Policy Statutes, p. 504; notes, pp. 505-506 (Foundation, 1985).

Problem 66

Todd has a fire policy with $25,000 worth of first party property coverage written by Mutual Ins. Co. The policy contained, the following clause:

> **Reduced rate contribution clause.** In consideration of the reduced rules and/or form under which this policy is written, it is expressly stipulated and made a condition of this contract that in the event of loss this Company shall be liable for no greater proportion thereof than the amount hereby assured bears to Seventy-Five Per Cent (75%) of the actual cash value of the property described herein.

Following a fire on Todd's premises, independent appraisers put the market value of Todd's property at $100,000 and estimate the total fire loss at $3000. What issues arise? What would you advise Todd as to the recovery he should expect under the policy?

PROBLEM 67

When Mary and Sam bought their home several years ago, the insurance policy which they purchased and still maintain contained the following clause:

> The Company shall not be liable for a greater proportion of any loss or damage to the subject property than the sum hereby insured bears to the percentage specified on the first page of this policy of the actual cash value of said property at the time of such loss, nor for more than the proportion which this policy bears to the total insurance thereon.

The face page of the policy contained the notation "Coinsurance Percentage--80%." Mary and Sam's home has appreciated since it was purchased.

Questions

1. Assume the actual cash value of the home at present is $100,000. Mary and Sam have $75,000 worth of insurance coverage. How much will they recover if they suffer a fire loss at this time and the actual cash value of the damage is:

   A. $100,000?

   B. $ 80,000?

   C. $ 30,000?

2. Assume the actual cash value of the home at present is $100,000. Mary and Sam have $80,000 worth of insurance coverage. How much will they recover if they suffer a fire loss at this time and the actual cash value of the damage is:

A. $100,000?

B. $ 80,000?

C. $ 30,000?

3. Assume the actual cash value of the home at present is $100,000. Mary and Sam have $90,000 worth of insurance coverage. How much will they recover if they suffer a fire loss at this time and the actual cash value of the damage is:

A. $100,000?

B. $ 80,000?

C. $ 30,000?

Notes

E. FISCHER & P. SWISHER, Principles of Insurance Law, *Schnitzer v. South Carolina ins. Co.*, p. 588; notes & questions, pp. 593-94 (Matthew Bender, 1986); R. HENDERSON, Insurance Law, "Policy Limits" and Other Pecuniary Limitations, p. 477; *Templeton v. Insurance Co. of North America*, p. 480; notes, p. 483 (Michie, 1989); R. JERRY, Understanding Insurance Law, §93[b] (Matthew Bender, 1987); R. KEETON & A. WIDISS, Insurance Law, §3.8 (West, 1988); R. KEETON, Basic Insurance Law, Excerpts, §3.7, pp. 199-202; *Jefferson Ins. Co. of N.Y. v. Superior Court*, p. 202 (West, 1977); A. WIDISS, Insurance, Coinsurance Provisions in Property Insurance, p. 181 (West, 1989); K. YORK & J. WHELAN, Insurance Law (Second Edition), Note, pp. 301-302; *Jefferson Insurance Co. v. Superior Court*, p. 302; notes, p. 305; *Apparel City Sewing Machine Co., Inc. v. Transamerica Ins. Group*, p. 305 (West, 1988); W. YOUNG & E. HOLMES, Insurance, Coinsurance, p. 506; notes, pp. 508-509 (Foundation, 1985).

E. Apportionment of Proceeds Among Various Interests

1. Life Tenants and Remainderpersons

Problem 68

Harriet Wilson owned her home, having outlived her husband. When she died, Harriet's Will left life estates in her property to her two sons, William and David, and the remainder in fee simple absolute to her daughter, Rebecca. The home has a value of $100,000.

Questions

1. Assume that after his Mother's death, William purchases an insurance policy for the full value of the house, naming himself as insured. The house is destroyed by fire. William, David and Rebecca each seek to collect their proportionate share under the policy. How much should each receive?

2. Assume instead that after William purchased the insurance in the preceding question, he and David were killed in a car wreck. Subsequently, the home is destroyed by fire and Rebecca seeks to recover the amount of the policy. What result?

3. Assume that David was killed in a car wreck; that William purchased insurance for the full value of the property and that William was killed in the fire which destroyed the property. How do you argue the case for Rebecca?

4. Assume that William, David, and Rebecca each purchase insurance for the full value of the property. After fire destroys the property, how much should each receive?

5. Assume that Rebecca purchases fire insurance, naming herself and her brothers as insureds. None of the three want to live in the house, however, and they agree to rent it to Tenant. How would you, on Tenant's behalf, negotiate the lease so as to protect your client in the event of a fortuitous fire?

6. Assume that Harriet had purchased insurance naming herself as the insured. Thereafter, she deeded the property over to the three children, equally, reserving to herself a life estate. Fire destroys the property. Who may collect on the insurance?

Problem 69

Following the death of his wife, Robert Dean deeded his farm property over to his three children, William, Sally and Anne, in equal shares. In the deed, Dean reserved to himself a life estate. Robert Dean was the only named insured on a property insurance policy written by Professional Farmers' Property and Casualty Co. That policy had a face amount of $150,000 and was written in a state which has a valued policy statute. Several weeks ago, the property was destroyed by explosion and subsequent fire. Professional Farmers' has sought your help on who, if anyone, to pay for the damage to the property.

Questions

1. Robert Dean was killed in the fire. It is unclear whether he died in the explosion or subsequent fire. For insurance purposes, what difference does it make?

2. Assume that Dean died with a Will which left all of his personal property to his local Church and that it has been determined that Dean lived through the explosion and died after the home had been substantially destroyed. Assume that the Professional Farmers' policy was a continuation of a policy which Dean had first purchased when he and his wife purchased the farm. The Church, William, Sally and Anne all claim an interest in the insurance proceeds. Who receives what?

3. Assume that Dean died with a Will which left all of his personal property to his local Church and that it has been determined that Dean lived through the explosion and died after the home had been substantially destroyed. Assume that the Professional Farmers' policy was a new policy which Dean had first purchased following his deed of the property to his children and the creation of the life estate for himself. The Church, William, Sally and Anne all claim an interest in the insurance proceeds. Who receives what?

4. Assume that the Court determines that William, Sally and Anne are all to share in the insurance proceeds. William also has a policy, to protect his remainder interest, with New Frontier Insurance, in the amount of $150,000. What are New Frontier's best arguments for not paying on William's claim.

5. Assume that Sally, hearing about the fire, has a heart attack and dies. Sally also had a property insurance policy with Property Plus Insurance, in the amount of $150,000. What are Property Plus' best arguments for not paying on Sally's claim?

Notes

E. FISCHER & P. SWISHER, Principles of Insurance Law, Morris v. Morris , p. 644; note, pp. 646-47 (Matthew Bender, 1986); R. HENDERSON, Insurance Law, *Morris v. Morris*, p. 404; note, p. 406 (Michie, 1989); R. JERRY, Understanding Insurance Law, §53D (Matthew Bender, 1987); R. KEETON & A. WIDISS, Insurance Law, §§4.4(c), 4.4(d) (West, 1988); R. KEETON, Basic Insurance Law, *Home Insurance Co. v. Adler*, p. 319; *Hunt v. General Ins. Co. of America*, p. 323; *In re Mullin's Estate*, p. 324 (West, 1977); K. YORK & J. WHELAN, Insurance Law (Second Edition), *Russell v Williams*, p. 313; *Sutton v. Jondahl*, p. 350; notes, p. 352 (West, 1988).

2. Mortgagors and Mortgagees

Problem 70

Sisters Tami and Dora Starkmond purchased a new home for $120,000 after first securing a $75,000 first mortgage from Third State Bank. As a condition of that mortgage, Tami and Dora applied for and received from Westfall Insurance Company a property insurance policy covering the property for the amount which Tami and Dora paid. The insurance policy was issued in the names of Tami and Dora Starkmond and listed Third State Bank as mortgagee. The policy provided:

> Loss, if any, under this policy, shall be payable to the mortgagee named on the first page of this policy, as its interest may appear, under all present or future mortgages upon the property ***.

The mortgage provided that default would occur if the Starkmonds failed to pay monthly installments on the loan or failed to pay real estate taxes or property assessments when they came due. Several years after moving in, the Starkmond property was damaged by fire. At the time, Tami and Dora still owed $70,000 on their mortgage, but the value of the home before the fire had increased to $140,000. The adjuster for Westfall Insurance estimated that the damage to the home was $50,000. After Tami and Dora found a contractor who would repair the home for that $50,000 amount, they learned that Third State claimed $25,000 under the insurance policy. Tami and Dora have remained current in their mortgage payments and would like to rebuild their house. How will the proceeds from the insurance be distributed?

Notes

K. YORK & J. WHELAN, Insurance Law (Second Edition), *Kreshek v. Sperling*, p. 323 (West, 1988).

PROBLEM 71

First Federal Property Insurance Company has traditionally offered two different types of insurance policies to its insureds whose properties are subject to outstanding mortgages. The first, known as the "Loss Payable Clause" provides as follows:

> If loss hereunder is made payable, in whole or in part, to a designated mortgagee not named herein as the insured, such

> interest in this policy may be cancelled by giving to such mortgagee a ten days' written notice of cancellation.

The other clause, known as a "Standard or Union Clause" provides as follows:

> Loss, if any, under this policy, shall be payable to the mortgagee named on the first page of this policy, as interest may appear, under all present or future mortgages upon the property herein described in which the aforesaid may have an interest as mortgagee in order of precedence of said mortgages; and this insurance as to the interest of the mortgagee shall not be invalidated by any act or neglect of the mortgagor or owner of the within described property, nor by any foreclosure or other proceedings or notice of sale relating to the property, nor by any change in the title or ownership of the property, nor by the occupation of the premises for purposes more hazardous than are permitted by this policy; provided that in any case the mortgagor or owner shall neglect to pay any premium due under this policy, the mortgagee shall, on demand, pay the same.

You have been asked to conduct a training program for new adjusters at First Statewide Insurance and are considering the result when loss to the property occurs, while Federal Savings and Loan Ass'n. is named as mortgagee in the policy, under the following circumstances:

Questions

1. Owner has a "Loss Payable Clause" and sells the house, without advising Federal Savings and Loan. Following the completed sale, fire destroys the house. Can Federal Savings and Loan collect under the policy?

2. Owner has a "Standard or Union Clause" and sells the house, without advising Federal Savings and Loan. Following the completed sale, fire

destroys the house. Can Federal Savings and Loan collect under the policy?

3. Owner has a "Loss Payable Clause." Owner is in default on the mortgage and mortgagee begins foreclosure proceedings. While these proceedings are pending, fire destroys the house. Can Federal Savings and Loan collect under the policy?

4. Owner has a "Standard or Union Clause." Owner is in default on the mortgage and mortgagee begins foreclosure proceedings. While these proceedings are pending, fire destroys the house. Can Federal Savings and Loan collect under the policy?

5. Owner has a "Loss Payable Clause." The foreclosure proceedings are final and the property is sold at a foreclosure sale. Following the sale, fire destroys the house. Can Federal Savings and Loan collect under the policy?

6. Owner has a "Standard or Union Clause." The foreclosure proceedings are final and the property is sold at a foreclosure sale. Following the sale, fire destroys the house. Can Federal Savings and Loan collect under the policy?

7. Owner has a "Standard or Union Clause." The foreclosure proceedings are final and the property is sold at a foreclosure sale to Federal Savings and Loan who is the high bidder at the sale. Following the sale, fire destroys the house. Can Federal Savings and Loan collect under the policy?

8. Owner has a "Loss Payable Clause" and the policy has been interpreted as excluding fires intentionally started by the insured. Insured intentionally burns the house down. Can Federal Savings and Loan collect under the policy?

9. Owner has a "Standard or Union Clause" and the policy has been interpreted as excluding fires intentionally started by the insured. Insured intentionally burns the house down. Can Federal Savings and Loan collect under the policy?

10. Owner has a "Loss Payable Clause" and owner fails to pay the premium on the policy, whereupon First Statewide sends 10 days notice of cancellation to Owner. The policy is cancelled and, thereafter, the house is destroyed by fire. Can Federal Savings and Loan collect under the policy?

Notes

E. FISCHER & P. SWISHER, Principles of Insurance Law, *Meade v. North Country Co-Operative Ins. Co.*, p. 635; notes & questions, pp. 638-39 (Matthew Bender, 1986); R. HENDERSON, Insurance Law, *Fields v. Western Millers Mut. Fire Ins. Co.*, p. 414; *Nationwide Mutual Fire Ins. Co. v. Wilborn*, p. 420; *Whitestone Savings & Loan Ass'n v. Allstate Ins. Co.*, p. 426; *Harvard Trust Co. v. Racheotes*, p. 427 (Michie, 1989); R. JERRY, Understanding Insurance Law, §53A (Matthew Bender, 1987); R. KEETON & A. WIDISS, Insurance Law, §4.2(a) (West, 1988); R. KEETON, Basic Insurance Law, *Grosvenor v. Atlantic Fire Ins. Co.*, p. 273; *Whitestone Savings & Loan Ass'n v. Allstate Ins. Co.*, p. 278; notes, pp. 285-86; *Fields v. Western Millers Mut. Fire Ins. Co.*, p. 286; *Ranger County Mutual Ins. Co. v. Chrysler Credit Corp.*, p. 291; *Harvard Trust Co. v. Racheotes*, p. 293, notes, pp. 294-95 (West, 1977); A. WIDISS, Insurance, Introductory Note, p. 274; *Burritt Mutual Savings Bank of New Britain v. Transamerica Ins. Co.*, p. 275 (West, 1989); K. YORK & J. WHELAN, Insurance Law (Second Edition), *Mann v. Glens Falls Insurance Co.*, p. 316; *Whitney National Bank of New Orleans v. State Farm Fire & Casualty Co.*, p. 320; problems, p. 323 (West, 1988); W. YOUNG & E. HOLMES, Insurance, *Mann v. Glens Falls Ins. Co.*, p. 463 (Foundation, 1985).

3. Landlord and Tenant

Problem 72

In a move designed to lessen traditional tension between Landlords and

Tenants, the Community Mediation Center has put together a workshop to explore the joint responsibilities, rights and obligations of the two parties to a lease. Included in the workshop are a number of insurance companies which write property insurance, both for landlords and for tenants. You have agreed to serve as moderator/legal consultant for the workshop. You anticipate that a hotly debated issue will be the liability of the respective insurers for landlord and tenant when both are insured, the property is damaged, and one or the other undertakes to repair the damage.

Questions

1. If the landlord has the obligation, under the lease, to repair any damage, does the tenant have an insurable interest sufficient to buy insurance for property damage?

2. If the landlord has the obligation, under the lease, to repair any damage, does the tenant have any loss when the property is damaged and the landlord repairs?

3. If the landlord has the obligation, under the lease, to repair any damage, how can the tenant collect on the tenant's insurance policy when the property is damaged and the landlord completes repairs?

4. If the tenant has the obligation, under the lease, to repair any damage, does the landlord have an insurable interest sufficient to buy insurance for property damage?

5. If the tenant has the obligation, under the lease, to repair any damage, does the landlord have any loss when the property is damaged and

the tenant repairs?

6. If the tenant has the obligation, under the lease, to repair any damage, how can the landlord collect on the landlord's insurance policy when the property is damaged and the tenant completes repairs?

Notes

E. FISCHER & P. SWISHER, Principles of Insurance Law, Parsons Manufacturing Corp. v. Superior Court , p. 621; notes & questions, pp. 639-40 (Matthew Bender, 1986); R. HENDERSON, Insurance Law, *Citizens Ins. Co. v. Foxbilt, Inc.*, p. 395; notes, pp. 399-400; Berman & Bourne, Renters Cope With Auto Cover Woes, p. 400; notes, pp. 403-404 (Michie, 1989); R. JERRY, Understanding Insurance Law, §53E (Matthew Bender, 1987); R. KEETON & A. WIDISS, Insurance Law, §§4.4(a), (b) (West, 1988); R. KEETON, Basic Insurance Law, *Wichita City Lines, Inc. v. Puckett*, p. 311; *General Mills, Inc. v. Goldman*, p. 314; *Citizens Ins. Co. v. Foxbilt, Inc.*, p. 315; *Ramsdell v. Insurance Co. of North America*, p. 318 (West, 1977); A. WIDISS, Insurance, Interests in Leased Property, p. 300; *Third Establishment, Inc. v. 1931 North Park Apts.*, p. 301 (West, 1989); K. YORK & J. WHELAN, Insurance Law (Second Edition), *Sutton v. Jondahl*, p. 350; notes, p. 352 (West, 1988); W. YOUNG & E. HOLMES, Insurance, Leases, p. 483; note, pp. 483-84; *Meadvin v. Buckley-Southland Oil Co.*, p. 484; notes, p. 486 (Foundation, 1985).

4. Vendor and Purchaser

Problem 73

Dave Davis owns a 10 acre plot of ground with some old currently unused farm buildings located thereon. Davis agrees to sell the land and buildings to Althea Johnson for $10,000 per acre or $100,000. Johnson plans to have her company, Johnson Enterprises, divide the land into 10 single acre parcel homesites. There are no contingencies in the contract and, in an effort to protect her interests, Johnson insures the property with 2D Insurance

Company in the amount of $100,000. Davis already has insurance with AAA Insurance, also in the amount of $100,000. While the sale is pending, fire destroys the buildings on the land.

Questions

1. If the contract of sale is silent on risk of loss, should Davis' insurance company be obligated to pay Davis and, if it does, does Johnson receive any benefit from that payment?

2. If the contract of sale is silent on risk of loss, should Johnson's insurance company be obligated to pay Johnson and, if it does, does Davis receive any benefit from that payment?

3. If the contract of sale is silent on risk of loss, can both Davis and Johnson each collect from their own insurance companies? What happens to the sale?

4. If the contract places risk of loss on seller until passing of title, should Davis' insurance company be obligated to pay Davis and, if it does, does Johnson receive any benefit from that payment?

5. If the contract places risk of loss on seller until passing of title, should Johnson's insurance company be obligated to pay Johnson and, if it does, does Davis receive any benefit from that payment?

6. If the contract places risk of loss on seller until passing of title, can both Davis and Johnson each collect from their own insurance companies? What happens to the sale?

Notes

E. FISCHER & P. SWISHER, Principles of Insurance Law, *Gilles v. Sprout*, p. 631; notes & questions, pp. 634-35 (Matthew Bender, 1986); R. HENDERSON, Insurance Law, *Brownell v. Board of Education*, p. 378; note, pp. 380-81; *Wolf v. Home Ins.*, p. 381; *Vogel v. Northern Assurance Co.*, p. 388; notes, p. 391; Risk of Loss Under the Uniform Commercial Code, p. 391; *Insurance Co. of North America v. Alberstadt*, p. 392; notes, p. 395 (Michie, 1989); R. JERRY, Understanding Insurance Law, §53B (Matthew Bender, 1987); R. KEETON & A. WIDISS, Insurance Law, §4.3 (West, 1988); R. KEETON, Basic Insurance Law, *Castellain v. Preston*, p. 298; *Brownell v. Board of Education*, p. 299; *Raplee v. Piper*, p. 300; *Vogel v. Northern Assurance Co.*, p. 302; *Paramount Fire Ins. Co. v. Aetna Casualty & Surety Co.*, p. 303; Purchase and Sale Transaction, pp. 310-11 (West, 1977); A. WIDISS, Insurance, Introductory Note, p. 290; *Tate v. Wood*, p. 291; *Smith v. Prudential Property & Cas. Co.*, p. 294; Allocation of the Risk of Casualty Loss as Between a Vendor and a Purchaser of Realty, p. 297 (West, 1989); K. YORK & J. WHELAN, Insurance Law (Second Edition), Insurance of Dual Interests Under Executory Land Sale Contracts--Preliminary Note, p. 328; Uniform Vendor & Purchaser Risk Act, p. 329; *Acree v. Hanover Ins. Co.*, p. 329; *Paramount Fire Insurance Co. v. Aetna Casualty & Surety Co.*, p. 332 (West, 1988); W. YOUNG & E. HOLMES, Insurance, *Brownell v. Board of Education*, p. 449; notes, pp. 452-53; *Acree v. Hanover Ins. Co.*, p. 453; notes, pp. 455-57; *Vogel v. Northern Assurance Co.*, p. 457; notes, pp. 460-63 (Foundation, 1985).

F. Subrogation

1. Procedural Issues

Problem 74

Following a high speed chase through several local neighborhoods, the police were finally able to corner Andre Hamilton after he crashed his car into the side of the house owned by Sam and Sarah Ocean. While Hamilton survived to stand charges, the Ocean home suffered $50,000 worth of structural damage. That damage was paid by PLA Property and Casualty Insurance Company, with whom the Oceans maintained their property insurance. You have been contacted by the adjuster for PLA, who has indicated that PLA would like to do whatever is necessary to collect the $50,000 paid on the Ocean claim back from Hamilton, who does have assets.

Questions

1. After review of the contract between PLA and Ocean, you find no clause indicating that subrogation rights exist between the two. Does PLA have any recourse?

2. Assume that the PLA/Ocean insurance contract does contain a clause which states: "The Company may require an assignment of rights of recovery for a loss to the extent that payment is made by us." When you contact the Oceans, however, they show no interest in aiding you or PLA in obtaining relief from Hamilton. Does PLA have any recourse?

Problem 75

Following an automobile accident in which she drove her car into the side of a parked car owned by Albert Davis, Sandy Alamos was sued by Carrier Mutual Insurance Company, the insurance company which wrote collision insurance on the other car. That suit sought $6,500 in damages to the other car. The suit was styled "*Albert Davis v. Sandy Alamos.*" In response to that suit, Sandy's lawyer has moved 1.) to dismiss the action for failure to name an indispensable party--Carrier Mutual, which will actually collect the money if there is a judgment against Sandy; or 2.) to join Carrier Mutual as a named plaintiff. What is the purpose of these motions and what will be the result of them?

Notes

E. FISCHER & P. SWISHER, Principles of Insurance Law, General Explanation of Subrogation, p. 599; *Commercial Union Ins. Co. v. Postin*, p. 599; notes & questions, p. 604; *Allstate Ins. Co. v. Town of Ville Platte*, p. 612 (Matthew Bender, 1986); R. HENDERSON, Insurance Law, *Skauge v. Mountain States Telephone & Telegraph Co.*, p. 108 (Michie, 1989); R. JERRY, Understanding Insurance Law, §§96[a], [b], [i] (Matthew Bender, 1987); R. KEETON & A. WIDISS, Insurance Law, §§3.10(a)(1), (c)(1),(4) (West, 1988); R. KEETON, Basic Insurance Law, *Hamilton Fire Ins. Co. v. Greger*, p. 244 (West, 1977); K. YORK & J. WHELAN, Insurance Law (Second Edition), *Wimberly v. American Casualty Co. of Reading, Pennsylvania (CNA)*, p. 361; *Paxton National Ins. Co. v. Brickajlik*, p. 371 (West, 1988).

2. Subrogation Against the Insured

Problem 76

Several months ago, Ralph Brill was cooking hamburgers on his charcoal grill which he had placed in his driveway. When it started to rain, Ralph gently moved the grill into the garage, careful to leave the garage door open. He placed the grill near where he was doing some woodworking. As the grease from the hamburgers began to flare in the grill, Ralph figured they were almost done and went inside to tell his wife that dinner was almost ready. Ralph did not see the gust of wind from the rainstorm catch the fire from the grease, send it into the wood that Ralph had been working on, and set fire to the entire house. The fire caused $30,000 worth of damage to the home, which was paid by First Sentry Insurance Co., Ralph's fire insurance carrier. That policy contains a provision which provides:

> SUBROGATION RIGHTS OF THE COMPANY: Whenever the company shall pay upon any loss of the insured, the Company may require an assignment of all right of recovery against any party for loss to the extent that payment therefore has been made by the Company.

First Sentry has now sent a letter to Ralph and his wife citing the subrogation clause and demanding $30,000 from them. What result? Why?

PROBLEM 77

As Student Legal Advisor to University Students at your State University, you regularly deal with landlord/tenant problems. As a result of increased incidents of smoking by students, especially during exams, there have been numerous fires in student-occupied rental housing. While the landlords have fixed up most of the premises, the students have been regularly sued by the landlords' insurance companies, who were obligated to pay for the losses. Your suggestion that students attempt to obtain their own insurance against property damage went generally unheeded, as most students could not afford the premiums on such a policy. You have now been asked by student leaders if you can suggest any modification of general lease agreements that would aid the students. Do you have any suggestions?

Notes

E. FISCHER & P. SWISHER, Principles of Insurance Law, *Reeder v. Reeder*, p. 605; notes, pp. 607-608 (Matthew Bender, 1986); R. JERRY, Understanding Insurance Law, §96[g] (Matthew Bender, 1987); R. KEETON & A. WIDISS, Insurance Law, §3.10(a)(1) (West, 1988); A. WIDISS, Insurance, Rules for Preventing Net Gain, p. 177; *Frank Briscoe Co., Inc. v. Georgia Sprinkler Co., Inc.*, p. 216;

Subrogation of the Lessor's Insurer to the Lessor's Claim for Indemnity Against the Tenant, p. 307; *Alaska Ins. Co. v. RCA Alaska Communications*, p. 307 (West, 1989); K. YORK & J. WHELAN, Insurance Law (Second Edition), *Cincinnati Insurance Co. v. Vulcan Materials Co., Inc.*, p. 353; *Frank Briscoe Co. v. Georgia Sprinkler Co.*, p. 355 (West, 1988).

3. Impairment of Subrogation Rights

Problem 78

About six months after purchasing their new home, Sandy and Ed Galwine sought a building contractor who would turn their existing single car garage into a family room and add a detached two car garage. After considerable searching, the Galwines chose the Kirkpatrick Construction Co. and entered into a contract for Kirkpatrick to complete the construct project at a cost of $20,000. While Kirkpatrick workers were removing the existing garage door on the home, a Kirkpatrick worker's unattended, but ignited acetylene torch set fire to the home, causing $50,000 worth of damage, including $10,000 worth of damage to the new garage. When they had first purchased the house, the Galwines had purchased insurance from Selected Markets Insurance Company for $80,000, which was the value of the home before any of the work was done. In reviewing the then pending building plans, the Galwine's insurance agent had estimated that the work would increase the value of the home to $110,000. That homeowner's policy continued in effect and had a clause which provided as follows:

SUBROGATION RIGHTS OF THE COMPANY: Whenever

> the company shall pay upon any loss of the insured, the Company may require an assignment of all right of recovery against any party for loss to the extent that payment therefore has been made by the Company.

Questions

1. Included in the contract negotiated between Galwine and Kirkpatrick Construction Co. was a clause which provided:

> In return for the lowered price at which this construction project is bid, Owner [Galwine] agrees to hold Contractor [Kirkpatrick] harmless for any act of negligence toward the subject property committed by Contractor.

Following the fire, Selected Risks refuses to pay on Galwine's claim alleging that Galwine impaired the subrogation rights of Selected Risks. Is this correct? Why or why not?

2. In the fire, Sandy Galwine sustained some injury. Following the fire, the Galwines were contacted by Sideline Insurance, the company representing Kirkpatrick Construction. The Galwines settled with Sideline, agreeing to accept $25,000 for the personal injuries of Sandy Galwine. In accepting that sum, the Galwines executed a release to Kirkpatrick and Sideline releasing both from any further liability, except as to the property damage. After that release was executed, Selected Risks again refused to pay Galwine for the property damage, claiming that Galwines impaired the subrogation rights of Selected Risks. Is this correct? Why or why not?

3. Assume that Selected Risks was willing to pay $40,000 (the damage

of \$50,000, less the \$10,000 worth of damage to the new construction which had not yet been added to the Selected Risks policy) and that the Galwines accepted this amount. The Galwines then sued Kirkpatrick Construction Co. directly for damages. In that action, Galwines were represented by an attorney who charged them a contingency fee of 40% of the net recovery. Filing fees in the action were \$60, and service of process fees were \$15. The Galwine's attorney hired a real estate expert to testify on the extent of damage to the overall home, based upon the damage to the addition. This expert charged \$150 for his report and \$250 to testify. The attorney also took depositions of the Kirkpatrick workers who were involved in the incident, and preparation of those depositions cost \$200. The jury awarded the Galwines the sum of \$13,000 in damages. Selected Risks now seeks reimbursement of \$3,000 which is claimed represents the difference between the \$40,000 paid by Selected Risks and the \$50,000 in damages. Is this correct? Why or why not?

Notes

E. FISCHER & P. SWISHER, Principles of Insurance Law, *Insurance Company of North America v. Abiouness*, p. 608; notes & questions, pp. 611-12 (Matthew Bender, 1986); R. JERRY, Understanding Insurance Law, §96[h] (Matthew Bender, 1987); R. KEETON & A. WIDISS, Insurance Law, §3.10(d) (West, 1988); R. KEETON, Basic Insurance Law, *Union Insurance Society v. Consolidated Ice Co.*, p. 239; *Holbert v. Safe Ins. Co.*, p. 243; *Hamilton Fire Ins. Co. v. Gregor*, p. 244; notes, p. 248; *Illinois Automobile Insurance Exchange v. Braun*, p. 248; notes, p. 249; *Great Northern Oil Co. v. St. Paul Fire & Marine Ins. Co.*, p. 249; notes, p. 254 (West, 1977); A. WIDISS, Insurance, Approaches to Allocating Recoveries Involving Subrogation, p. 224; Enforcement of Subrogation Rights; p. 225 (West, 1989); K. YORK & J. WHELAN, Insurance Law (Second Edition), *Stetina v. State Farm Mutual Auto Ins. Co.*, p. 364; *Home Ins. Co. v. Hertz Corp.*, p. 369; *Executive Jet Aviation, Inc. v. United States*, p. 372 (West, 1988).

4. Subrogation in Mortgagor/Mortgagee Cases

Problem 79

Sometime after Roland James purchased his home, he discovered the tax aspects of home ownership and decided to purchase a second home for vacationing on the Maine coast. Both homes were financed, his residence with First National Bank and his vacation home with Second National Bank. Because they were purchased at different times and were located in different states, Roland insured the properties with different insurance companies. His residence was insured with Homeowners National Insurance Company, for the full $100,000 value of the home. The policy listed First National Bank as mortgagee and then contained a clause, which the policy called "Loss Payable" and which provided:

> If loss hereunder is made payable, in whole or in part, to a designated mortgagee not named herein as the insured, such interest in this policy may be cancelled by giving to such mortgagee a ten days' written notice of cancellation.

The vacation home Roland insured with Ocean Atlantic Insurance Co., also for the full $75,000 value of the home. That policy had a clause which was titled "Standard Clause" and provided:

> Loss, if any, under this policy, shall be payable to the mortgagee named on the first page of this policy, as interest may appear, under all present or future mortgages upon the property herein described in which the aforesaid may have an interest as mortgagee in order of precedence of said mortgages; and this

> insurance as to the interest of the mortgagee shall not be invalidated by any act or neglect of the mortgagor or owner of the within described property, nor by any foreclosure or other proceedings or notice of sale relating to the property, nor by any change in the title or ownership of the property, nor by the occupation of the premises for purposes more hazardous than are permitted by this policy; provided that in any case the mortgagor or owner shall neglect to pay any premium due under this policy, the mortgagee shall, on demand, pay the same.

In addition, both policies provided that in the event any payment was made under the policy, the insurance company would be subrogated to the rights of any party paid.

Questions

1. Assume that Roland James sold his vacation home, without advising Second National. Within a week after the sale was complete, the home burned to the ground. After paying Second National, Ocean Atlantic seeks to enforce its subrogation rights. What result?

2. Assume that Homeowners National cancels the insurance policy on Roland's residence because Roland refused to pay the premium. Homeowners cancelled by sending Roland a notice of cancellation. Following cancellation, the house burned as a result of a negligent act by a third party. Homeowners was compelled to pay First National on its claim for the damage. Is Homeowners National subrogated?

3. Assume that Roland set fire to the vacation home because the area in which it was located had been overrun by tourists. After paying Second

National, Ocean Atlantic seeks reimbursement from Roland. What result? Why?

Notes

E. FISCHER & P. SWISHER, Principles of Insurance Law, *Twin City Fire Ins. Co. v. Walter B. Hannah, Inc.*, p. 616; notes & questions, pp. 619-620 (Matthew Bender, 1986); R. JERRY, Understanding Insurance Law, §96[a] (Matthew Bender, 1987); R. KEETON & A. WIDISS, Insurance Law, §§4.2(b), (c), (d), (e), (f) (West, 1988); R. KEETON, Basic Insurance Law, *Grosvenor v. Atlantic Fire Ins. Co.*, p. 273; *Whitestone Savings & Loan Ass'n v. Allstate Ins. Co.*, p. 278; notes, p. 285-86; *Fields v. Western Millers Mut. Fire Ins. Co.*, p. 286; *Ranger County Mut. Inc. Co. v. Chrysler Credit Corp.*, p. 291; *Harvard Trust Co. v. Racheotes*, p. 292; notes, pp. 294-95 (West, 1977); A. WIDISS, Insurance, *Dalrymple v. Royal Globe Ins. Co.*, p. 282; note, Standard (Union) Mortgage Clauses, p. 284 (West, 1989); K. YORK & J. WHELAN, Insurance Law (Second Edition), *Mann v. Glens Falls Ins. Co.*, p. 316; *Whitney National Bank of New Orleans v. State Farm Fire & Casualty Co.* p. 320 (West, 1988).

5. Subrogation Under No Fault Legislation

Problem 80

The new European luxury car owned by Barbara Banks was struck as it sat, unoccupied, in the parking lot adjoining Barbara's office. The driver of the car which struck Barbara's car, Leon Carter, fled the scene, but was eventually caught and admitted the collision. The damage to Barbara's car was extensive and repairs totaled $10,000. Barbara made a claim for those damages under what she thought was the "collision" portion of her automobile insurance policy with National Auto Insurance Exchange. As it turns out, Barbara's state legislature had adopted a Motor Vehicle Accident Reparations Act (No-Fault). The No-Fault legislation required all automobile insurance policies to provide for "compensation, without regard to fault for damage to the insured motor vehicle, subject to deductions at the option of the insured." The legislation then provided:

> Insurers providing benefits in this state without regard to fault for damages to the motor vehicle shall not be subrogated to the rights of the person for whom benefits are provided, except in those motor vehicle accidents involving two or more vehicles where 1.) one of the vehicles has a gross weight in excess of 6,500 pounds or 2.) where the driver of one of the vehicles is an Uninsured Motorist; or 3.) where failure to permit subrogation would result in double recovery for the insured.

After paying all of Barbara's $10,000 repair bill, less the $100 deductible contained in the policy, National Auto seeks to enforce the provision of the contract which provides:

> SUBROGATION RIGHTS OF THE COMPANY: Whenever the company shall pay upon any loss of the insured, the Company may require an assignment of all right of recovery against any party for loss to the extent that payment therefore has been made by the Company.

Questions

1. Can National Auto seek to collect the amount paid on Barbara's claim from Carter? Why or why not?

2. Under the statutory scheme, can National refuse to include No-Fault "collision" coverage in its policies?

3. If a right of subrogation were to exist, could National Auto allege

that it is inapplicable if Barbara refuses to institute suit against Carter?

4. Who is the real party in interest in a subrogation case in a No-Fault state?

5. Assume that Barbara lived in the state adjoining the state wherein the accident took place and that National Auto wrote the insurance contract in the adjoining state. Barbara's home state does not have No-Fault legislation. When Barbara is involved in the accident with Carter in a state with No-Fault, but is insured by an insurer from a state without No-Fault, does subrogation arise?

Notes

R. HENDERSON, Insurance Law, *Cirelli v. Ohio Casualty Ins. Co.*, p. 114; notes, pp. 117-18 (Michie, 1989); A. WIDISS, Insurance, *Allstate Ins. Co. v. Reitler*, p. 227; *Sturiano v. Brooks*, p. 352 (West, 1989).

Chapter Six

Personal (Life and Health) Insurance

A. Insurable Interest

Problem 81

Alice is Bert's sister. Alice is the sole beneficiary under a policy of life insurance taken out on Bert's life. Alice and Bert have had no contact for the last five years aside from three acrimonious phone conversations. Alice has a 5% share-holding in the corporation of which Bert is the chief operating officer. Bert dies. Can Alice recover under the life policy? What additional information do you require? What issues arise and how will they be resolved?

PROBLEM 82

John and Sue had been friends for all the years they could remember. Their parents lived next door, they went to the same schools, and attended the same college. They knew each other's habits, thoughts, emotions and had always relied on each other's judgment in times of crisis. When they were both 21 and about to graduate from college and, after having a few too many beers one night, they decided to place a value on their friendship. After much wrangling, they decided that they could not realistically estimate how much each would miss the society, companionship and comfort of each other, but decided that it would be worth at least $50,000. The next day, they decided to insure their friendship and each purchased $50,000 worth of life insurance on the life of the other naming the survivor beneficiary. The Insurance was purchased from the Old Reliable Insurance Company. Following graduation, John and Sue drifted apart geographically, but stayed in communication. At their fifth year college reunion, both John and Sue came alone and on that night realized that neither could ever marry anyone but the other. As a result they were married shortly thereafter. The next year, Sue died during the birth of their first child. Old Reliable has refused to pay on the insurance John purchased on Sue claiming absence of insurable interest. Discuss.

PROBLEM 83

Mary Webster met Andy Mirriam at a meeting of Parents Without Partners.

Both divorced with children from prior marriages, they fell immediately in love and, after a one year courtship, were married. Mary had two children; David Webster, age 21, who was living on his own; and Andrea Webster, age 18, at college, but living at home. After the marriage, Andy Mirriam did not adopt either of these children. David Webster was distrustful of his mother's second husband and was nervous about his mother's financial security. As a result, he applied for and was issued a $200,000 insurance policy written on his step-father's life by the Monarch Insurance Company. David named his mother as beneficiary, although he never told her about the policy. Following the untimely death of Andy Mirriam, David, on his mother's behalf, submitted an appropriate proof of loss to Monarch Insurance Company, but that Company refused to pay indicating an absence of insurable interest.

Questions

1. If Monarch Insurance Company refuses to pay, will David, on his mother's behalf, be able to collect over a claim of absence of insurable interest?
2. Suppose the policy itself had a clause which provided as follows:

> "INCONTESTABLE: After this policy has been in full force and effect for two years during the lifetime of the Insured, it shall become incontestable as to the statements contained in the original application." Assume that Andy Mirriam lived for 3 years after the policy issued. Following Andy's death, will David be able to collect the proceeds for his mother?

Problem 84

The Windy Candle Partnership holds the music publishing interests and property in master recordings for some 1970's pop music. Bernie and Reggie, the two partners, contemplate that the partnership will be dissolved within the next ten years. As a matter of fact they no longer work together and have kept the partnership intact for sentimental reasons and a few minor tax advantages. Their advisers have suggested that, for investment purposes, they should each take out $2 million in term life insurance on the life of the other.

Questions

1. Following Reggie's death, the insurance company refuses payment to Bernie based upon the absence of insurable interest? What result?

2. Do you have any recommendations as to what Bernie and Reggie could have done to avoid any potential insurable interest problems?

Problem 85

Harry has a total annual income of $10,000. Harry's wife asked him to sign an insurance form. Under the mistaken belief that it was for automobile insurance, Harry signed what turned out to be an application for life insurance which included $500,000 of accidental death coverage on Harry. The annual premium for this coverage was $7,500.

Harry became suspicious of his wife after discovering a copy of the life policy. He contacted the insurance company and asked them where it had come from. Long Life replied that they would get back to him. Two months later, Harry's wife tried to stage a boating accident and kill him, but Harry survived.

Harry brings suit against Long Life Insurance.

Questions

1. Assess the relative merits of the following arguments made by Harry:

a) His wife has no insurable interest in Harry's life and the policy should be declared void.

b) A triable issue existed on the question whether Harry had given his consent to the taking out of the policy.

c) A triable issue existed on the question whether Long Life had actual knowledge of a plot to kill Harry that should have triggered an investigation by the defendant.

d) A triable issue existed on the question whether Long Life was negligent in failing to investigate the disproportion between the amount of premium and Harry's income.

2. What effect should be given to obtaining of the insured's consent before a policy issues?

3. Suppose Harry had been a minor and the policy had been taken out by his legal guardian who later attempted to murder him. What effect would a specific statutory provision attempting to protect a minor have on the recognition of a common law action for "endangerment of the insured?"

4. If the attempt on Harry's life had been successful, could his estate have collected on the policy?

Notes

E. FISCHER & P. SWISHER, Principles of Insurance Law, Who Has an Insurable Interest in a Life?, p. 123; *Rubenstein v. Mutual Life Ins. Co. of N.Y.*, p. 124; notes & questions, p. 129; *Peeler v. Doster*, p. 129; notes & questions, pp. 132-33; *Wren v. New York Life Ins. Co.*, p. 134; notes & questions, pp. 137-38; Patterson, Essentials of Insurance Law, pp. 137-38; *Amalgamated Labor Life Ins. Co. v. Rowe*, p. 138; Who May Question the Existence of Insurable Interest, p. 140; *Ryan v. Tickle*, p. 140; notes & questions, pp. 142-43; *American Casualty Co. v. Rose*, p. 143; notes & questions, p. 146; *Albrent v. Spencer*, p. 151; notes & questions, p. 154 (Matthew Bender, 1986); R. HENDERSON, Insurance Law, *Mutual Savings Life Ins. Co. v. Noah*, p. 28; *Lynch v. Bogenrief*, p. 32; *Lakin v. Postal Life & Cas. Co.*, p. 33; notes, pp. 35-38; *Dalby v. The India & London Life Ass. Co.*, p. 39; notes, pp. 43-45; *Liberty National Life Ins. Co. v. Weldon*, p. 45 (Michie, 1989); R. KEETON & A. WIDISS, Insurance Law, §§3.3, 3.5 (West, 1988), R. JERRY, Understanding Insurance Law, §§44; 45 (Matthew Bender, 1987); R. KEETON, Basic Insurance Law, Statutes, pp. 155-59; *Dalby v. The India & London Life Assurance Co*, p. 171; *Secor v. Pioneer Foundry Co*, p. 176; Insurable Interest at What Time, pp. 182-83; *McCluskey v. Providence Washington Ins. Co.*, p. 183; *Womble v. Dubuque Fire & Marine Ins. Co.*, p. 183 (West, 1977); A. WIDISS, Insurance, Introductory Note, p. 147; *Dalby v. The India & London Ass. Co.*, p. 148; *Graves v. Norred*, p. 158 (West, 1989); K. YORK & J. WHELAN, Insurance Law (Second Edition), Statutes, pp. 412-13; note, pp. 413-414; *Mutual Savings Life Ins. Co. v. Noah*, p. 414; *New England Mutual Life Ins. Co. v. Null*, p. 417; *Secor v. Pioneer Foundry Co.*, p. 514; Buy-Sell Agreements--Insurance Aspects, pp. 518-520 (West, 1988); W. YOUNG & E. HOLMES, Insurance, *Burton v. John Hancock Mut. Life Ins. Co.*, p. 526; The Tort of Insuring, p. 529; *Dixon v. Western Union Ass. Co.*, p. 531; notes, pp. 531-32; Statutes, pp. 532-34; Assignment & Insurable Interest, p. 535; Secor v. Pioneer Foundry Co. , p. 545; Cessation of Ins. Interest, p.545; Contrasting Rules, pp. 546-47; note, p. 548 (Foundation, 1985).

B. Warranties, Representations, Concealment

Problem 86

Arthur Dullard applied for a $250,000 life insurance policy with Suspicious Insurance. He was examined by Mr. Glove, a company nurse, who also asked him a long list of complicated questions about his medical history and any present symptoms. Specifically, Arthur was asked whether he had ever suffered from liver or kidney ailments or had been treated for substance abuse. Arthur answered in the negative to these questions. However, Glove noted on the application form that Arthur was very nervous and had excessively dilated pupils. When Glove complained that some of his answers were less than clear, Dullard replied that he could always contact St. Bernard's Hospital in Kansas and ask Dr. Jones, his urologist there. Glove made a cursory attempt to find the hospital and doctor but had no success.

Dullard's application was nonetheless approved by Suspicious' medical examiner without any further investigation and the policy was thereafter issued. Dullard subsequently died of complications associated with total renal failure as a result of chronic alcohol abuse. Suspicious has declined to pay on the policy, having discovered that Dullard had spent two months in the care of a Dr. Johnson at St. Bernard's alcohol rehabilitation center in Springfield, Missouri about six months prior to his application to Suspicious.

Questions

1. Should Dullard's wife, Claire, (designated as beneficiary in the policy) be allowed to collect? Why or why not?

2. Assume that Arthur Dullard's kidney disorder had gone into remission and that he had died after a kidney bean lodged in his throat and he choked to death. How do your arguments change?

3. Assume that Dullard's kidney disorder had gone into remission and

that he had gotten drunk at a party, fell into a kidney-shaped swimming pool and drown. How do your arguments change?

4. Assume that Dullard's kidney disorder had, in fact, gotten worse (indeed terminal) but that Dullard had been told by his doctor that he was in remission and had nothing to worry about. How do your arguments change?

5. Assume that in his original application, Dullard gave Mr. Glove the exact address of St.Bernard's hospital and Dr. Johnson and a complete truthful report from both St. Bernards and Dr. Johnson on the extent of Dullard's condition. Glove refused to read the report or contact either St. Bernards or Dr. Johnson. How do your arguments change?

6. Assume that, at the time the insurance was applied for, Dullard was accompanied by his wife, Claire, who had already spoken at length to Dr. Johnson. She thus knew that Dullard's days were indeed numbered and that only a short period of time would pass before Dullard would be required to be hospitalized for the final time. Indeed it was Claire Dullard who encouraged Arthur to apply for the insurance. The remaining facts in the main problem do not change except that Claire offered no comment when Arthur gave Glove the wrong location for both St. Bernard's Hospital and Dr. Johnson. Claire, however, was asked no questions either by Glove or the Agent who completed the application form. Following Arthur's death, you may assume that the insurer found out that Claire had far more knowledge than she had volunteered. Can Claire collect on the policy? Why or why not?

Notes

E. FISCHER & P. SWISHER, Principles of Insurance Law, *Bankers Life & Cas. Co. v. Long*, p. 241; notes & questions, pp. 244-46; Reliance By the Insurer, p. 259; McGill, Life Insurance, p. 269; (Matthew Bender, 1986); R. HENDERSON, Insurance Law, *New York Life Ins. Co. v. Miller*, p. 836; notes, pp. 840-42; *New York Life Ins. Co. v. Strudel*, p. 842; *Berger v. Minnesota Mut. Life Ins. Co.*, p. 847; notes, pp. 850-53; statutes, pp. 862-64; notes, pp. 864-65 (Michie, 1989); R. JERRY, Understanding Insurance Law, §§101-103 (Matthew Bender, 1987); R. KEETON & A. WIDISS, Insurance Law, §§5.6-5.8 (West, 1988); R. KEETON, Basic Insurance Law, *New York Life Ins. Co. v. Strudel*, p. 531; *Columbian Nat. Life Ins. Co. v. Lanigan*, p. 537; *Stecker v. American Home Fire Assurance Co.*, p. 539; *Blair v. National Security Ins. Co.*, p. 543; *Penn Mutual Life Ins. Co. v. Mechanics' Savings Bank & Trust Co.*, p. 544; *Harte v. United Benefit Life Ins. Co.*, p. 551; *Harte v. United Benefit Life Ins. Co.*, p. 555; *Praetorian Mutual Life Ins. Co. v. Sherman*, p. 661; *John Hancock Mutual Life Ins. Co. v. Conway*, p. 665; *New York Life Ins. Co. v. Kuhlenschmidt*, p. 678; *Penn Mutual Life Ins. Co. v. Mechanics' Savings Ban & Trust Co.*, p. 687 (West, 1977); A. WIDISS, Insurance, Insurance Policy Provisions and Legal Consequences, p. 520; *Berthiaume v. Minnesota Mut. Life Ins. Co.*, p. 522; Concealment, p. 537; Introductory Note, p. 701; Statutes Concerning Warranties, Representations, and Concealment, p. 702 (West, 1989); K. YORK & J. WHELAN, Insurance Law (Second Edition), Statutes, pp.100-103; notes, pp. 103-105; *Funchess v. United States Life Ins. Co.*, p. 105; notes, pp. 106-107; *Thompson v. Occidental Life Ins. Co.*, p. 107; note, pp. 112-13; *Lettieri v. Equitable Life Assurance Society of U.S.*, p. 113 (West, 1988); W. YOUNG & E. HOLMES, Insurance, Warranties & Life Insurance, p. 177; *Friesz v. National Old Line Ins. Co.*, p. 178; *Countryside Casualty Co. v. Orr*, p. 181; notes, pp. 186-88; statutes, pp. 188-181; notes, pp. 191-93; *Friesz v. National Old Line Ins. Co.*, p. 194; *Mooney v. Underwriters at Lloyds*, p. 195; Standards of Materiality, p. 201; Proof of Materiality, p. 203; notes, pp. 203-204; A Concealment Case, p. 204; notes, pp. 205-206 (Foundation, 1985).

C. Coverage Issues

1. Incontestability

Problem 87

Anne Marie Olsen purchased a combination life and health insurance policy from Guardian Life and Health Insurance Co. Before she did, she filled out an application form for the company which included a number of health-related questions. Among those questions was one which asked: "Has applicant ever suffered from or been diagnosed as having *** Acquired Immune Deficiency Syndrome (AIDS)?" Tired of people asking her about AIDS, Anne Marie answered "No" to this question, despite the fact that she had been diagnosed as being an AIDS carrier 3 years previously and had been undergoing testing 3 times a year since that time to determine if she had become actively infected with the disease. When the policy issued, it issued at Guardian's regular rates, instead of the greatly increased premium rate which Guardian would have charged if it knew that Anne Marie was a diagnosed AIDS carrier. The policy had the application filled out by Anne Marie attached to it, but also contained the following provision:

> "INCONTESTABLE--This policy shall be incontestable as to any statements contained in the application therefore after the policy has been in force during the lifetime of the insured for a period of two years from the effective date of the policy." The policy insured against medical expenses and provided for a lump sum death benefit if the expense (or death) resulted from a "covered sickness." The policy then defined "covered sickness" as "any sickness, injury, or illness which first manifests itself during the term of this policy."

Questions

1. One year after the policy issued, Guardian Life and Health learned that Anne Marie had been previously diagnosed as an AIDS carrier. At the time it so learned, Anne Marie was up-to-date in premium payments and had made no claims on the insurance. What options are open to the Company?

What will be the result of the exercise of any of these options?

2. Eighteen months after the policy issued, and before Guardian discovered Anne Marie's previous diagnosis, Anne Marie was struck by a truck, hospitalized, and died as a result of her injuries 5 days later. Must Guardian pay for the hospital and doctor bills and pay the death benefit?

3. Twenty six months after the policy issued, and before Guardian discovered Anne Marie's previous diagnosis, Anne Marie became actively infected with AIDS. She was hospitalized and eventually died. Must Guardian pay for the hospital and doctor bills and pay the death benefit?

4. Thirty months after the policy issued, and before Guardian discovered Anne Marie's previous diagnosis, Anne Marie was struck by a truck, hospitalized, and died as a result of her injuries 5 days later. Must Guardian pay for the hospital and doctor bills and pay the death benefit?

Notes

E. FISCHER & P. SWISHER, Principles of Insurance Law, Incontestability Provisions, p. 260; *White v. Massachusetts Cas. Ins. Co.*, p. 260; notes & questions, p. 262; *Burnham v. Bankers Life & Cas. Co.*, p. 263 (Matthew Bender, 1986); R. HENDERSON, Insurance Law, *Crawford v. Equitable Life Ass. Society of U.S.*, p. 872; notes, pp. 879-81 (Michie, 1989); R. JERRY, Understanding Insurance Law, §104B (Matthew Bender, 1987); R. KEETON & A. WIDISS, Insurance Law, 3.3(c), 6.6(d) (West, 1988); R. KEETON, Basic Insurance Law, *Metropolitan Life Ins. Co. v. Conway*, p. 630; notes, pp. 632-33 (West, 1977); A. WIDISS, Insurance, *Searle v. Allstate Life Ins. Co.*, p. 468; Incontestability Provisions, p. 710 (West, 1989); K. YORK & J. WHELAN, Insurance Law (Second Edition), *Massachusetts Casualty Ins. Co. v. Forman*, p. 432 (West, 1988); W. YOUNG & E. HOLMES, Insurance, Incontestability, p. 226; *Metropolitan Life Ins. Co. v. Conway*, p. 227; notes, pp. 229-230; *Simpson v. Phoenix Mut. Life Ins. Co.*, p. 230 (Foundation, 1985).

2. "Reasonable Medical Expenses"

Problem 88

Our client, Loving Family Health Insurance Company, uses the following language in its health insurance policy:

> Reimbursable medical expenses are reasonable charges which the insured (as defined) actually has incurred for services performed or drugs or medicines furnished at the instruction of the insured's attending physician provided that such services are medically necessary.

Loving Health's claims adjusters have referred the following files to us for evaluation. The insureds in each case have submitted documented claims for reimbursement for all noted procedures and attendant expenses. Which, if any, of the claims should be paid? Why?

(A) Mrs. Johnson was diagnosed as suffering from cancer. She underwent all conventional procedures including chemotherapy. After these procedures proved unsuccessful, she went to a private research center in the Caribbean where she underwent a course of intramuscular injections of certain immune serum proteins. This procedure was not approved other than for experimental purposes in the United States. Mrs. Johnson reported that she felt much better following the treatment.

(B) Mr. Basil is treated for a renal complaint by Dr. Dill, his long-standing physician. Dr. Dill is a qualified and board certified urologist who also practices holistic medicine. Dr. Dill prescribed Mr. Basil a course of care and treatment which included minerals, herbs and nutritional supplements.

(C) Mr. Slight, 65 years of age and the victim of severe osteoarthritis, suffered his second bruising fall in a period of three weeks. He was in a frail condition and had a history of suffering from blackouts. There was no one to care for him at his home. His doctor hospitalized him for ten days.

(D) Mrs. Petri was diagnosed as infertile. She underwent a procedure known as tuboplasty in an attempt to repair her fallopian tubes. This procedure was unsuccessful. She was referred by her physician to an infertility clinic where her child was conceived using an *in vitro* fertilization process.

(E) Ms. Crash is involved in a minor automobile accident. She suffers considerable soft tissue injuries. She undertakes thermographic diagnosis. Thermography measures infrared radiation emanating from the skin and, according to some physicians, renders an accurate visual image of the patient's pain. These "pain pictures" are frequently utilized by attorneys in making claims against automobile insurers.

Notes

R. HENDERSON, Insurance Law, *Connecticut General Life Ins. Co. v. Shelton*, p. 226; notes, pp. 232-34 (Michie, 1989); R. KEETON, Basic Insurance Law, *Mason v. Loyal Protective Life Ins. Co.*, p. 497 (West, 1977); A. WIDISS, Insurance, *Stanley v. Safeco Ins. Co. of America*, p. 408 (West, 1989); K. YORK & J. WHELAN, Insurance Law (Second Edition), *Chalmers v. Metropolitan Life Ins. Co.*, p. 445 (West, 1988).

3. Other Coverage Clauses

Problem 89

Marty Bush and his wife, Amelia both got out of work early one day and met at a local bar. In fact, they spent much of the afternoon and early evening drinking in the bar and by 10:00 p.m., all evidence was that both were inebriated. At about 10:00 p.m., an argument broke out between Marty and Amelia and Amelia stormed out of the bar. Marty stormed out after her indicating, by gesture, that he intended to harm his wife. Evidently frightened by her husband's actions, Amelia jumped into the family car and attempted to drive out of the bar's parking lot. Apparently further enraged by his belief that his wife was leaving him, Marty jumped on to the hood of the car and attempted to hold on while lying spread-eagle on the hood. When she saw her husband do this, Amelia immediately applied the brakes to stop the car. Instead of helping the situation, this action by Amelia caused Marty to fly off the car, land against a fence surrounding the parking lot, and shatter his leg.

By this time, Jim Davis, the bartender at the bar, had come into the parking lot. Though not required by his job to investigate such incidents, Davis knew both Marty and Amelia and sensed that neither should be driving. As Davis saw Marty fly through the air, Davis began running to help, unaware that he was running directly in front of another vehicle exiting the parking lot. Davis was struck by that other vehicle and sustained a serious head injury.

Questions

1. You should assume that Jim Davis was denied worker compensation benefits for his injuries because chasing after patrons was outside the scope of his employment. Davis then made a claim on a health insurance policy he owned. That policy exempted from coverage "any injury arising out of, or in the course of, any employment for wage or profit;" and, as a result, the company refuses coverage. What result? Who bears the risk of non-persuasion?

2. Davis had another injury as well. When he was thrown to the ground, he permanently injured the cornea of his right eye causing his vision in that eye to deteriorate to 2/200 without glasses. With glasses, vision returns to 20/30 but remains difficult in dim light. Davis' health policy will pay a specified amount ($10,000) for "loss of sight in one eye." Again, the company refuses to pay. What result? Who bears the risk of non-persuasion?

3. Marty Bush was hospitalized for the damage to his leg and as a result was in traction for a period of three weeks. As a result of being confined to bed for that period of time, Bush developed a blood clot in his leg. That clot remained undiagnosed and Bush was discharged from the hospital. Exactly 9 weeks after he was discharged, that same blood clot shot from Bush's leg to his brain and killed him. Bush had a life insurance policy which paid his estate $50,000 upon his death, but which paid $100,000 if Bush's death "occurs within 60 days of any accident." The company now refuses to pay anything. What result? Who bears the risk of non-persuasion?

4. As it turns out, Bush was diagnosed, some 5 years before the policy

in the preceding question was obtained, as having high blood pressure and had been taking medicine since that diagnosis designed to thin his blood. Bush had stopped taking the medicine while he was in the hospital, because he was feeling better. Failure to take the medicine can result to clotting. Bush was covered by a second health/life insurance policy which exempted from coverage any claim "caused or contributed to by any preexisting bodily or mental infirmity, condition, or illness." This company takes the position that the blood clot was caused by the high blood pressure and refuses to pay a death benefit. What result? Who bears the risk of non-persuasion?

5. As a result of the death of her husband, which she believes that she caused, Amelia Bush has found that she simply cannot drive an automobile. While she has no physical ailments, her mental state simply makes it impossible for her to climb behind the wheel. Prior to this incident, Amelia had been a highly successful life insurance salesperson and had done substantial traveling, primarily by automobile. While she was a member of the College of Life Underwriters, Amelia had little other training outside of insurance sales. She is covered by a disability insurance policy which will pay her a disability income if she "is totally disabled so as to be unable to engage in any gainful occupation or employment for which she is reasonably qualified by education, training, or experience." The insurance company refuses to recognize Amelia as disabled. What result? Who bears the risk of non-persuasion?

PROBLEM 90

Bluto was attending college at the Allstate Valley Institute of Technology. He was a pledge at the Phi Phe Phum fraternity. On Hell Night Bluto consumed approximately one gallon of home brewed beer. He lost consciousness and fell out of a second story window of the fraternity house. He was rushed to hospital with a serious head wound and given a blood transfusion. Unfortunately, the blood was contaminated and Bluto died two days later. Knowing that their son was going to be attending college, Bluto's parents had taken out an accident policy on him with Neverpay Insurance. The insuring clause in that policy stated:

> We will pay benefits under this policy only if the death of the insured is a result of bodily injuries effected through external, violent and accidental means.

An exclusionary clause was to the effect that:

> We will not pay benefits under this policy when the death of the insured is caused by or results from sickness or disease or medical or surgical procedures or treatment.

Neverpay refused coverage when Bluto's parents claimed the accidental death benefits under the policy.

Questions

1. What issues arise? How would you expect them to be resolved?

2. Suppose that Bluto had been under treatment for alcoholism since his fifteenth birthday. Would a pre-existing condition exclusion apply?

Notes

E. FISCHER & P. SWISHER, Principles of Insurance Law, *Sekel v. Aetna Life Ins. Co.*, p. 423; notes & questions, p. 426; Semantic Distinction Theories, p. 426; *Spaid v. Cal-Western States Life Ins. Co.*, p. 427; *Moore v. American United Life Ins. Co.*, p. 429; notes & questions, p. 435 (Matthew Bender, 1986); R. HENDERSON, Insurance Law, *Crobons v. Wisconsin National Life Ins. Co.*, p. 213; notes, p. 219; *Deschler v. Fireman's Fund American Life Ins. Co.*, p. 219; *Prudence Life Ins. Co. v. Wooley, p. 223; notes, pp. 225-26* (Michie, 1989); R. Jerry, Understanding Insurance Law, §§63C; 64 (Matthew Bender, 1987); R. KEETON & A. WIDISS, Insurance Law, §§5.4(b), (c) (West, 1988); R. KEETON, Basic Insurance Law, *Burr v. Commercial Travelers Mut. Accident Ass'n*, p. 481; *Silverstein v. Metropolitan Life Ins. Co.*, p. 487; *Bernhard v. Prudential Ins. Co.*, p. 496 (West, 1977); K. YORK & J. WHELAN, Insurance Law (Second Edition), *Massachusetts Casualty Ins. Co. v. Forman*, p. 432; *Willden v. Washington National Ins. Co.*, p. 437; *Strickland v. Gulf Life Ins. Co.*, p. 440; notes, pp. 444-45; *Chalmers v. Metropolitan Life Ins. Co.*, p. 445; *Arata v. California-Western States Life Ins. Co.*, p. 448 (West, 1988); W. YOUNG & E. HOLMES, Insurance, Notes, pp. 221-22; The Safecracker's Case, p. 223 (Foundation, 1985).

4. "ACCIDENT"(AL) ISSUES

PROBLEM 91

Recently retired from her position as chair of the Department of Romantic Studies at State University, Sebrina Leonard decided to go into business for herself and she opened a small record store specializing in rock and roll oldies from the 1950's, 60's and 70's. Sebrina's store opened at the time when most single recordings were being offered on compact disc so that the rock and roll staple, the 45 r.p.m. record was an idea whose time had pretty well come and gone. As a result, sales were thin, although after about a year, Sebrina had developed a loyal clientele of Oldies' fans so that the idea of a profit was not longer totally out of the question. Unfortunately, however, such notions evaporated the day that two patrons got into a heated discussion over whether Gerry and the Pacemakers were better than Herman's Hermits, a discussion which soon erupted into a fight which resulted in the police having to be called to restore calm and which destroyed about 60% of Sebrina's Oldies' collection. The next day, Sebrina's body was found on the street in front of her store. The available evidence is in conflict: One purported eye witness saw a woman who looked like Sebrina standing in the window on the third floor above her store. The witness then turned away and heard the sound of screeching tires, turned and saw Sebrina fly through the air and land on the hood of a passing station wagon. Another witness claims to have seen Sebrina leave the store and walk into the street, where she was struck by the station wagon, thrown into the air and land on the hood. The driver of the station wagon does not know what happened and first saw Sebrina in the air. Sebrina was covered by two life insurance policies, each in the amount of $100,000.

Questions

1. The first policy was purchased by Sebrina a year before her death and just after she retired from the University and opened her record store. It contained a clause which provided as follows: "SUICIDE CLAUSE--If the Insured commits suicide, while sane or insane, within two years from the date coverage begins under this policy, payment by the Company shall be limited to a return of any unearned premium." The Company has refused payment under this policy. What result? Who bears the risk of non-persuasion?

2. Assume that Sebrina was involuntarily retired from the University following threats she made against students and that she had been diagnosed as a paranoid schizophrenic and given medication therefore. This illness was disclosed to the insurer who wrote the insurance policy in the preceding question. Shortly before her death, Sebrina stopped taking the medication. The witness who claimed that Sebrina walked from the store into the street has now recanted and recalls seeing Sebrina screaming obscenities about how the world was out to get her from the third floor window above the store just before she jumped. As a result, the Company refuses to pay on the insurance. What result? Who bears the risk of non-persuasion?

3. The other insurance policy was taken out by Sebrina some 5 years prior to her death while still a University employee. It also had a Suicide Clause identical to the one above. The policy was titled "Accidental Death" policy and provided for payment only in the event that "death is caused by accident." The Company refuses to pay on this insurance. What result? Who bears the risk of non-persuasion?

4. Assume that the facts ultimately reveal that Sebrina was murdered by one Jerry Mercer, a spurned lover of Sebrina's and one of the combatants in the Record Store fight, who was enraged that Sebrina had called the police, thereby jeopardizing Mercer's probationary status. Mercer followed Sebrina to the Record Store the next day; held her hostage, dragged her up to the third floor and pitched her out the window. Mercer has a $75,000 life insurance policy on himself.

A. Assume that Mercer slipped while pitching Sebrina out the window and also fell to his death. Will his policy pay the named beneficiary? Why or Why not?

B. Assume that Mercer had a fatal heart attack as a result of carrying Sebrina up the stairs and throwing her out the window. His life insurance policy excludes coverage for "death resulting from criminal activity." Will his policy pay the named beneficiary? Who bears the risk of non-persuasion?

C. Assume that Mercer lives and is caught. He stands trial, is convicted and sentenced to death for his crimes. Pursuant to that sentence, Mercer is executed by the State for his activity. Will his policy pay the named beneficiary? Why or Why not?

Notes

1. Further Accident(al) problems are contained in Chapter 7, section C.

2. E. FISCHER & P. SWISHER, Principles of Insurance Law, "Accident, Accidental Death, Accidental Means," p. 411; *Burr v. Commercial Travelers Mut. Accident Assoc.*, p. 411; notes & questions, p. 414; *Hearn v. Southern Life & Health Ins. Co.*, p 414; notes & questions, p. 422 (Matthew Bender, 1986); R. HENDERSON , Insurance Law, *INA Life Ins. Co. v. Brundin*, p. 149; notes, pp. 155-56; *Kasper v. Provident Life Ins. Co.*, p. 156; notes, pp. 159-160; *Hoffman v. Life Ins. Co. of North America*, p. 160; notes, pp. 169-170; *Carter v. Carter*, p. 370; *Nielsen v. Provident Life & Acc. Co.*, p. 881 (Michie, 1989); R. JERRY, Understanding Insurance Law, §§63B[a], [b]; 63C[d] (Matthew Bender, 1987); R. KEETON & A. WIDISS, Insurance Law, §§5.3(b), (c) (West, 1988); R. KEETON, Basic Insurance Law, *Burr v. Commercial Travelers Mutual Accident Ass'n.*, p. 481; *Silverstein v. Metropolitan Life Ins. Co.*, p. 487; *Mohn v. American Casualty Co. of Reading*, p. 490; *Bernhard v. Prudential Ins. Co.*, p. 496; (West, 1977); A. WIDISS, Insurance, *Fehring v. Universal Fidelity Life Ins. Co.*, p. 396; Implied Exceptions to Life Ins., p. 428; *Harper v. Prudential Ins. Co. of America*, p. 430; *Wilkins v. Fireman's Fund American Life Ins. Co.*, p. 450; *Hearn v. Southern Life & Health Ins. Co.*, p. 458; *Fryman v. Pilot Life Ins. Co.*, p. 461; *Bigelow v. Berkshire Life Ins. Co.*, p. 464; *Searle v. Allstate Life Ins. Co.*, p. 468; *Gottfried v. Prudential Ins. Co. of America*, pp. 484, 489, 495 (West, 1989); K. YORK & J. WHELAN, Insurance Law (Second Edition), *Knight v. Metropolitan Life Ins. Co.*, p. 450; *Wetzel v. Westinghouse Electric Corp.*, p. 455; notes, pp. 458-465 (West, 1988); W. YOUNG & E. HOLMES, Insurance, *Roque v. Nationwide Mutual Ins. Co.*, p. 269; Notes, pp. 270-72; The Additional Clause, p. 272 (Foundation, 1985).

E. Payment of Proceeds

Problem 92

David has two children by his marriage to Rachel. In a divorce proceeding between David and Rachel, support of the two children is an issue. David has a $1 million life insurance policy on himself which had named Rachel as beneficiary prior to the break-up of the marriage.

Questions

1. Assume that David and Rachel agree, in a written property settlement agreement, that David will name the two children as beneficiaries of the $1 million life policy. David does not, later marries Elizabeth, names Elizabeth as beneficiary and dies. Both Elizabeth and Rachel, as Guardian of the two children, claim the proceeds. What result? Why?

2. Assume that you represent the Insurance Company which issued the $1 million policy. You are in receipt of two proofs of death; one filed by Elizabeth attaching a copy of the policy showing her as beneficiary; and one filed by Rachel, attaching a copy of the signed Settlement Agreement. What options are open to the Company? If you file a lawsuit, does the Company give up any rights to later challenge, for example, warranties made by David?

3. Assume that David and Rachel did not enter into a property settlement agreement but that the Judge who heard the divorce case Ordered

David to make the children beneficiaries as part of the Court's determination of an equitable distribution of the property of the couple. Does your answer to Question 1 change? Why?

PROBLEM 93

Sandra owned a life insurance policy in the amount of $50,000 issued by Security Life and Casualty Co. When she purchased the policy, Sandra named her parents as beneficiaries. Following her marriage to Andrew, a marriage not at all favored by her parents, Sandra wrote and sent a letter to Security Life in which she requested that the beneficiary on the policy be changed to "my husband, Andrew J. Wiggins." Sandra received a letter from the Company indicating that she had to fill out and return a Company Change of Beneficiary Form. Shortly thereafter, Sandra was killed in an airplane crash. In her top dresser drawer was the completed, but as yet, unmailed Change of Beneficiary Form. Who is entitled to the proceeds?

PROBLEM 94

When Debbie purchased her brand new Porsche 944 Turbo the finance company wanted her assurance that she had sufficient life insurance so that the vehicle could be paid for in the event of Debbie's demise. As a result, Debbie executed an assignment of her $75,000 whole life policy with New Jersey Life Ins. Co. to Finance Company. Thereafter, Finance Company named itself as beneficiary. Shortly thereafter, Debbie won the lottery and enough money so that she fully paid off her loan. She then wrote to New Jersey Life stating: "Please be advised that I wish to change the beneficiary of Whole Life Policy #345-8210 back to me as the loan for which the policy was serving as security has now been fully paid." New Jersey Life, which accepts changes of beneficiary by letter from the insured, ignored this letter. Debbie died while a passenger in another car and her estate seeks the proceeds from the New Jersey Life policy. What result? Why?

Problem 95

Taylor obtained a policy of life insurance on his own life from Delta Federal Life Insurance Company, naming his brother, Chuck, as beneficiary. Subsequently, Taylor assigned the policy to Annie, a longtime business partner, who changed the beneficiary to herself. After Annie lost an ugly struggle for control of their jointly owned business, she murdered Taylor. Taylor is survived by his brother, Chuck, and three minor children of a dissolved marriage. Who should receive the proceeds? How, procedurally, can your result be accomplished?

Notes

E. FISCHER & P. SWISHER, Principles of Insurance Law, Problems with Change of Beneficiaries, p. 653; *Travelers Ins. Co. v. Smith*, p. 654; notes & questions, p. 656; *Equitable Life Assurance Soc. v. Stitzel*, p. 657; notes & questions, 659-660; *Bourne v. Haynes*, p. 662; notes & questions, p. 663 (Matthew Bender, 1986); R. HENDERSON, Insurance Law, *Lemke v. Schwarz*, p. 353; notes, pp. 356-57; *Davis v. Modern Industrial Bank*, p. 357; notes, pp. 361-62; *Aetna Life Ins. Co. v. Wadsworth*, p. 362; notes, pp. 369-370 (Michie, 1989); R. JERRY, Understanding Insurance Law, §§52; 52A; 52B; 98 (Matthew Bender, 1987); R. KEETON & A. WIDISS, Insurance Law, 3.5(b), (c), (d), (e), (f) (West, 1988); R. KEETON, Basic Insurance Law, *Secor v. Pioneer Foundry Co.*, p. 176; *Gigsby v. Russell*, p. 184; *Butterworth v. Mississippi Valley Trust Co.*, p. 186; *Langford v. National Life and Accident Ins. Co.*, p. 187; *Warnock v. Davis*, p. 188; *Bromley's Administrator v. Washington Life Ins.*, p. 189; *Hack v. Metz*, p. 190; *Liberty National Life Ins. Co. v. Weldon*, p. 191; *Mollett v. United Benefit Life Ins. Co.*, p. 382; *Katzman v. Aetna Life Ins. Co.*, p. 385; *Davis v. Modern Industrial Bank*, p. 392; *Beneficial Life Ins. Co. v. Stoddard*, p. 398; *Stone v. Stephens*, p. 400; *United States v. Pahmer*, p. 401; *Albrent v. Spencer*, p. 402; *Albrent v. Spencer*, p. 405; *Carter v. Carter*, p. 406; *Minasian v. Aetna Life Ins. Co.*, p. 414 (West, 1977); A. WIDISS, Insurance, *Empire Life Ins. Co. v. Moody*, p. 152; *New York Life Ins. Co. v. Baum*, pp. 161, 165; *Bacon v. Federal Kemper Life Ass. Co.*, p. 169; Identifying the Insureds in Life Insurance, p. 268; *Lightner v. Centennial Life Ins. Co.*, p. 269; Introductory Note to Life Insurance, pp. 379-382; *Provident Mut. Life Ins. Co. v. Ehrlich*, p. 383; *New York Life Ins. Co. v. Henriksen*, p. 392; *Meir v. New Jersey Life Ins. Co.*, p. 581 (West, 1989); K. YORK & J. WHELAN, Insurance Law (Second Edition), *Leonard v. Occidental Life Ins. Co.*, p. 468; notes, pp. 471-72; *Occidental Life Ins. Co. of California v. Row*, p. 472; *Manhattan Life Ins. Co. v. Barnes*, p. 476; notes, pp. 480-83; *Commissioner v. Noel Estate*, p. 484; *Life & Casualty Ins. Co. v. Martin*, p. 487; notes, pp. 489-490 (West, 1988); W. YOUNG & E. HOLMES, Insurance, *Travelers Ins. Co. v. Smith*, p. 548; notes, pp. 551-53; The Beneficiary's Interest, p. 553; notes, pp. 554-55; *New York Life Ins. Co. v. Henriksen*, p. 555; notes, p. 559 (Foundation, 1985).

F. Subrogation

Problem 96

William had a health insurance policy which paid reasonable medical and hospital expenses. The policy also paid a lump sum of $100,000 in the event that William died as a result of an accident. William was injured, hospitalized and subsequently died after being struck by Milton Lush, a drunk driver, while William was attempting to cross the street pursuant to a "walk" signal. William had reasonable medical and hospital expenses of $13,800 prior to his death. The Insurance Company has paid that amount and, additionally, has paid William's estate the lump sum of $100,000.

Questions

1. Assume the policy contains no provisions regarding subrogation. What arguments can be made both for and against subrogation claims by the insurer?

2. Assume the policy contains the following clause: "In the event of any payment under this policy, the company shall be subrogated to all the insured's or beneficiary's right of recovery therefor against any person ***." Are there any problems with enforcing this clause against Lush, who was insured at the time of the loss?

3. Assume the policy contains the following clause: "In the event of payment under this policy, the company shall be subrogated to the extent of such payment to the proceeds of any settlement or judgment that results from the exercise of any rights of recovery which the insured or beneficiary may have against any person ***." Are there any problems with enforcing this clause against an insured Lush?

Notes

R. HENDERSON, Insurance Law, *Cunningham v. Metropolitan Life Ins. Co.*, p. 85; notes, pp. 94-96; *Morin v. Massachusetts Blue Cross, Inc.*, p. 96; notes, pp. 103-104; *State Farm Mut. Auto. Ins. Co.*, p. 104; notes, pp. 107-108 (Michie, 1989); R. JERRY, Understanding Insurance Law, §96 (Matthew Bender, 1987); R. KEETON & A. WIDISS, Insurance Law, §§3.10(a)(6), (7), (8) (West, 1988); R. KEETON, Basic Insurance Law, *Michigan Hospital Service v. Sharpe*, p. 219; *Morin v. Massachusetts Blue Cross, Inc.*, p. 226; *State Farm Mutual Automobile Ins. Co. v. Pohl*, p. 235 (West, 1977); A. WIDISS,

Insurance, Introductory Note to Subrogation, p. 210; *Blue Cross and Blue Shield of Wisconsin v. Fireman's Fund Ins. Co.*, p. 211; Note: "Conventional" & "Legal" Subrogation, p. 215; *American Pioneer Life Ins. Co. v. Rogers*, p. 221 (West, 1989); K. YORK & J. WHELAN, Insurance Law (Second Edition), *Lee v. State Farm Mutual Ins. Co.*, p. 491; notes, pp. 495-96; *Matter of Estate of Schmidt*, p. 497; note, pp. 498-500 (West, 1988); W. YOUNG & E. HOLMES, Insurance, Subrogation & Bodily Injury Claims, p. 411; notes, pp. 413-14 (Foundation, 1985).

Chapter Seven

Liability Insurance Generally

A. Presentation of Claims

Problem 97

On the evening of November 4, two years ago, Bill Cason was out driving with his girlfriend Karen Wade. Cason, who was sixteen at the time, was driving his father's new sports car with his father's permission. At a street corner, Cason and Wade met Doug Gimbel, another 16 year old, who was driving another new sports car of a different manufacturer. When the light changed, both drivers attempted to get ahead of the other on the two lane road and a race resulted with Cason on the right side of the road and Gimbel on the left side of the road. As they approached an intersection, Cason and Gimbel both saw a car coming to the intersection from the side street to their left. That car turned right immediately into the path of the Gimbel car, with a resulting head-on collision between the two vehicles which took Gimbel's life. Cason heard the sound of breaking glass and Wade looked around to see that an accident had taken place, but both Cason and Wade continued down the street. Cason admitted to friends the next day, in response to their statements to him that Gimbel had been killed, that he was going about 95 mph when he left Gimbel. Cason did not admit then, nor to anyone thereafter, that he had been present when the accident took place. Last year, Gimbel's estate filed a lawsuit against the driver of the turning car, who claims to have no recollection of the events. Called to a deposition some 6 months ago, Cason finally admitted that he had been racing with Gimbel and that he had seen the turning car before it turned. The attorney for the turning driver advised Cason at that time that the attorney would seek to add Cason as a third-party defendant to the law suit.

The car driven by Cason was owned by and insured by his father, with whom Cason did and still does live, under a policy which included as insured: "The named insured and residents of the household of the named insured." The policy also contained the following:

> 8. When an accident occurs, written notice shall be given by the insured to the company as soon as is practicable. Such notice shall contain particulars sufficient to identify the insured and also reasonably obtainable information respecting the time, place and circumstances of the accident, the names and addresses of the injured and of available witnesses.
>
> * * *
>
> 12. No action shall lie against the company unless, as a condition precedent thereto, the insured shall have fully complied with all of the terms of this policy.

When Cason advised the insurer after the deposition of what was said,

Cason was told that he would not be covered by the company because of his failure to provide timely notice.

Questions

1. What is the purpose of the Notice provision of the policy and is there any difference between its purpose and the purpose of similar notice provisions in property and health insurance?

2. What is the meaning of "as soon as practicable?"

3. Suppose notice was given to the insurance company by the lawyer for Gimbel's estate with a copy of the police report? Suppose notice was given by the Turning Driver? Cason's Father?

4. Who bears the ultimate risk of non-persuasion on the issue?

Notes

E. FISCHER & P. SWISHER, Principles of Insurance Law, Notice of Loss Requirements, p. 485; *Miller v. Dilts*, p. 485; notes & questions, pp. 488-89; *Goodwin v. Nationwide Ins. Co.*, p. 489; notes & questions, pp. 491-92 (Matthew Bender, 1986); R. HENDERSON, Insurance Law, *Siravo v. Great American Ins. Co.*, p. 647; notes, pp. 652-54 (Michie, 1989); R. JERRY, Understanding Insurance Law, §81 (Matthew Bender, 1987); R. KEETON & A. WIDISS, Insurance Law, §§7.2(a)-(e), (g) (West, 1988); R. KEETON, Basic Insurance Law, *Members Mutual Ins. Co. v. Cutaia*, p. 787; note, p. 791 (West, 1977); A. WIDISS, Insurance, Introductory Note, p. 717; Claims Presentment, p. 719; Provisions Requiring Notice, p. 720; *Brakeman v. Potomac Ins. Co.*, p. 722; *Lord v. State Farm Mut. Ins. Co.*, p. 729 (West, 1989); K. YORK & J. WHELAN, Insurance Law (Second Edition), *Security Mutual Ins. Co. of New York v. Acker-Fitzsimons Corp.*, p. 523; notes, pp. 526-28 (West, 1988); W. YOUNG & E. HOLMES, Insurance, *Great American Ins. Co. v. C.G. Tate Construction*, p. 326; notes, pp. 331-32 (Foundation, 1985).

B. Exceptions, Occurrences, Exclusions

1. "Occurrence(s)"

Problem 98

Several years ago, Marilyn Roberts noticed a small lump on her left breast. When she brought it to the attention of her gynecologist, Dr. Evelyn Turnower, the doctor looked at the lump, felt it and assured Marilyn that there was no problem. As the lump got larger, Marilyn became more concerned. She went back to Dr. Turnower who diagnosed the lump as excessive milk in the gland. A year later, Marilyn insisted on a biopsy of the lump, which was done. Although the pathology report clearly indicated a malignancy, Dr. Turnower misread it and told Marilyn the lump was benign. Consequently, when surgery was performed two months later to remove the "benign" lump, Dr. Turnower was unprepared for the scope of the malignancy that she found. As a result, subsequent surgery was needed to attempt to remove as much of the cancer as possible. After this second surgery, Dr. Turnower wrote a note to set up Chemotherapy for Marilyn, but then put the note in the file of another patient. It was thus another 6 months before Chemotherapy was begun. Marilyn Roberts died from her cancer two months later. Her family has sued Dr. Turnower.

Questions

1. Assume that Dr. Turnower had one malpractice insurance policy throughout these events. The policy, in the amount of $25,000 for each claim, insured against "all sums which the insured shall become legally obligated to pay as damages because of injury to which this insurance applies caused by an occurrence, in the practice of the insured's profession." "Occurrence" is defined

as "any act or omission in the furnishing of professional medical service." How many occurrences took place for which a separate $25,000 maximum is available?

2. Assume that Dr. Turnower changed insurers just after she misread the pathology report on Marilyn Roberts. Her old insurance policy provided coverage for "occurrences within the policy period." Does this policy cover the claim by the estate of Marilyn Roberts?

3. Assume that in a new insurance policy which she purchased just after the death of Marilyn Roberts, Dr. Turnower purchased coverage for "occurrences" defined as "any act or omission in the furnishing of professional medical service which, results, during the policy period, in bodily injury or death." Does this policy cover the claim by the estate of Marilyn Roberts?

4. Assume that the actions of Dr. Turnower did not occur to Marilyn Roberts, but instead, the same misdiagnosis and failure to properly read a pathology report occurred on David Calvin, a 3 month old child. David did not die, but wound up with astronomic hospital and doctor bills and was disfigured for life. He eventually filed suit within 2 years after his 18th birthday, as required by state statute. What issues of insurance coverage are involved?

PROBLEM 99

Twenty-four years ago, Robert Blissful, under contract with the City of Eldon Beach, brought in 50 truckloads of fill dirt and spread that dirt over various City parks, including baseball diamonds and areas over which tennis courts were later built. Blissful had purchased the dirt from J.D. Excavating

Co., which had originally removed the dirt from the former site of Waste Management Corp., whose factory was torn down and excavated by J.D. Excavating. Waste Management knew that it had a large quantity of toxic wastes which it had stored in drums behind the plant. Many of those drums leaked and the spillage was absorbed into the ground. The dirt taken from the site and placed on the ground at Eldon Beach has now been found to contain a deadly toxic substance. All research indicates that it is the ultimate by-product of the original Waste Management dumping. While they had insurance during the period the factory was open, Waste Management went out of business 10 years ago and insurance was discontinued. J.D. Excavating was forced into Bankruptcy 5 years ago and, as a result, its insurance was not renewed by either the Trustee in bankruptcy or the subsequent owner of a reorganized D. & J. Excavating Contractors. Robert Blissful had business insurance for all of the years that he was in business. That policy was, however, discontinued when Blissful simply ceased operation several years ago.

Questions

1. Assume that all of the insurance policies held by Waste Management Corp., J.D. Excavating and Blissful provided for coverage for an "occurrence, which results, during the policy period, in bodily injury or property damages neither expected nor intended from the standpoint of the insured." From which Insurer can the injured residents of Eldon Beach expect compensation?

2. Assume that the policies instead defined "Occurrence" as "an accident which results in bodily injury or property damages neither expected nor intended from the standpoint of the insured." Is there coverage?

3. Assume that the policies instead defined "Occurrence" as "an accident, during the policy period, which results in bodily injury or property damages neither expected nor intended from the standpoint of the insured." Is there coverage?

4. Assume that the policies instead defined "Occurrence" as "an accident, which results, during the policy period, in bodily injury or property damages neither expected nor intended from the standpoint of the insured." Is there coverage?

5. Assume that the policies instead defined "Occurrence" as

> "an accident, including injurious exposure to conditions, which results, during the policy period, in bodily injury or property damages neither expected nor intended from the standpoint of the insured."

Is there coverage?

6. Assume that the policies instead defined "Occurrence" as

> "an accident, including injurious exposure to conditions, which results in bodily injury or property damages neither expected nor intended from the standpoint of the insured."

Is there coverage?

Problem 100

Jane Alberts was sued by David Johnson and his parents, Mr. and Mrs. Alvin Johnson, as a result of injuries to David in an automobile accident. Jane was driving her car, with David as a passenger when she lost control of the vehicle and crashed it into a bridge abutment. David, then age 16, was substantially injured, suffering permanent injury to his back. He was confined to a hospital for 8 months, had to have private duty nurses, and his injuries necessitated substantial remodeling of the Johnson home. The law suit sought damages for David's personal injuries and sought compensation for the medical and additional expenses expended by David's parents. Jane Albert has automobile insurance which pays $50,000 per person and $100,000 per occurrence for "each occurrence" covered by the policy. Jane's insurance company concedes liability to David for $50,000 but resists any further obligation. What result?

Notes

E. FISCHER & P. SWISHER, Principles of Insurance Law, Insurer's Liability for Progressive Injuries--Products Liability, §5.08, pp. 457-480; *Home Indemnity Co. v. City of Mobile*, p. 533; notes & questions, p. 537 (Matthew Bender, 1986); R. JERRY, Understanding Insurance Law, §65[a] (Matthew Bender, 1987); R. KEETON & A. WIDISS, Insurance Law, §§5.9, 5.10(d) (West, 1988); R. KEETON, Basic Insurance Law, *Argonaut Southwest Ins. Co. v. Maupin*, p. 449; *Olsen v. Moore*, p. 558; *Gyler v. Mission Ins. Co.*, p. 571 (West, 1977); A. WIDISS, Insurance, *Michigan Chemical Corp. v. American Home Ass. Co.*, p. 551; *Applachian Ins. Co. v. Liberty Mutual Ins Co.*, p. 571 (West, 1989); K. YORK & J. WHELAN, Insurance Law (Second Edition), *Olsen v. Moore*, p. 548; notes, p. 553; *Appalachian Ins. Co. v. Liberty Mutual Ins. Co.*, p. 554; problems, pp. 559-560; Note, Adjudicating Asbestos Insurance Liability: Alternatives to Contract Analysis, pp. 560-64; notes, pp. 564-65; *American Home Products Corp. v. Liberty Mutual Ins. Co.*, p. 565 (West, 1988); W. YOUNG & E. HOLMES, Insurance, Asbestosis, p. 367; notes, p. 369; *Keene Corp. v. Insurance Co. of North America*, p. 369; notes, 371-74 (Foundation, 1985).

2. *"Bodily Injury" and "Damages"*

PROBLEM 101

Randolph Gates, Professor of Law at Private University, told Brenda Starr, a second semester third year law student enrolled in his seminar and whom Gates knew was happily married, "Brenda, if you don't have sex with me, I will fail your seminar paper." Brenda refused, but because she was fearful of

Gates' reputation in the Law School and University, also refused to report Gates' statement. As a result, Starr was not aware that the University was already keeping a file of such complaints against Gates. Unfortunately, but also as a result, Brenda found that she was unable to continue with her legal studies. She fell behind in all of her courses, was unable to enroll in another seminar and eventually dropped out of law school after her faculty advisor told her that the faculty would not likely waive its long time seminar as a prerequisite to graduation requirement. Starr thus gave up the $50,000 per year Associate position she had already accepted at a major law firm. Instead, Brenda took a job as a junior high English teacher. Brenda sued Gates and Private University for intentional infliction of emotional distress. A jury believed Brenda and her evidence and awarded her $350,000 in compensatory damages against Gates; $200,000 compensatory damages against the University; and $1,000,000 in punitive damages against both. Both Gates and the University were defended in the action by attorneys for their respective Insurance companies, after those companies had conducted an investigation and found that, even if Gates knew his conduct was improper and knew that it would have some adverse effect on Brenda Starr, he did not think that she would drop out of school as a result of the threat which he indeed intended to carry out.

Questions

1. Assume that Gates' Homeowners insurance policy provided, under the liability protection provisions: "We will pay all sums which the insured is legally obligated to pay as a result of bodily injury or property damage caused by the insured." Will this Insurance company be obligated to pay all or a part

of the compensatory or punitive damage award?

2. Assume that Private University has a liability insurance policy which provides for coverage for "all sums which the insured is legally obligated to pay." Will this Insurance company be obligated to pay all or a part of the compensatory or punitive damage award?

Problem 102

Drain was dismissed from his lucrative investment banking position after a stock market crash. After he filed an unsuccessful suit against his ex-employer alleging wrongful discharge, his ex-employer instituted an action for malicious prosecution against Drain. Drain requested that his homeowner's insurance carrier, Doubtful Insurance Co., defend him. After initially accepting the defense subject to a reservation of rights, Doubtful informed Drain that exclusions in the homeowners's policy negated coverage and filed this action for declaratory relief.

The Doubtful Insurance coverage was its standard homeowners policy and provided:

> The Company agrees to pay on behalf of the Insured all sums which the Insured becomes legally obligated to pay as damages because of bodily injury or property damage, to which this insurance applies * * *

Doubtful Insurance moves for summary judgment, arguing that there is no potential for liability under the policy. Who should win? Why?

Notes

E. FISCHER & P. SWISHER, Principles of Insurance Law, Insurer's Liability for Punitive Damages, p. 444; *Hensley v. Erie Ins. Co.*, p. 444; *U.S. Concrete Pipe Co. v. Bould*, p. 448; notes & questions, p. 451 (Matthew Bender, 1986); R. HENDERSON, Insurance Law, *First Bank (N.A.)-Billings v. Transamerica Ins. Co.*, p. 205; notes, pp. 212-13 (Michie, 1989); R. JERRY, Understanding Insurance Law, §65[f] (Matthew Bender, 1987); R. KEETON & A. WIDISS, Insurance Law §§5.3(g), 5.4(d), (e) (West, 1988); R. KEETON, Basic Insurance Law, *Southern Farm Bureau Casualty Ins. Co. v. Daniel*, p. 440; (West, 1977); A. WIDISS, Insurance, Liability Insurance, p. 332; Liability Insurance Coverage for Punitive Damages, p. 441; *U.S. Concrete Pipe Co. v. Bould*, p. 442 (West, 1989); K. YORK & J. WHELAN, Insurance Law (Second Edition), notes, pp. 543-48 (West, 1988); W. YOUNG & E. HOLMES, Insurance, *Perl v. St. Paul Fire & Marine Ins. Co.*, p. 103; *Greenwood Cemetery, Inc. v. Travelers Indemnity Co.*, p. 294; notes, pp. 297-99; *Dayton Hudson Corp. v. American Mutual Liability*, p. 299; notes, pp. 305-306; *Public Service Mut. Ins. Co. v. Goldfarb*, p. 306; notes, p. 308 (Foundation, 1985).

3. Causation Problems Generally

Problem 103

April Goodall, then age 35, was babysitting for Michael Johnson, age 3, when Michael fell out of the crib where he was taking a nap, resulting in severe injuries. April was paid $2.00 per hour for babysitting Michael, and worked for Mrs. Johnson on an irregular basis about 15-20 hours per week. Usually, April worked for Mrs. Johnson while April was also watching her own daughter, May. In fact, at the time of the accident to Michael, May was sleeping in an adjoining crib. April has a homeowners insurance policy which provides the following:

> This policy does not apply:
>
> e. to injury or damage arising out of business pursuits of the Insured other than activities which are ordinarily incident to non-business pursuits ....

Now sued for negligence by the Johnsons, April would like to know if her homeowner's policy will cover her for alleged negligent babysitting? What other facts would assist your analysis?

Notes

R. KEETON & A. WIDISS, Insurance Law, §5.5 (West, 1988); A. WIDISS, Insurance, *Economy Fire & Cas. Co. v. Bassett*, p. 75 (West, 1989).

4. *"Arising Out of ****"*

PROBLEM 104

Little Sarah Fleming was bitten by Sparky, a French poodle owned by Joe Vader. Little Sarah was Sparky's third biting victim that month. At the time of the accident the dog was with Vader at Empire Incorporated, the toy business of which he was the president.

Following suit filed by Sarah against Vader, an action for a declaration as to coverage was brought by Frogstar Insurance who had provided Vader with homeowner's coverage.

The Frogstar policy contained, the following clauses:

This policy does not apply:

> e. to injury or damage arising out of business pursuits of the Insured other than activities which are ordinarily incident to non-business pursuits;
>
> * * *
>
> h. to injury or damage which is either expected or intended from the standpoint of Insured.
>
> * * *
>
> j. to injury or damage arising out of any premises other

than the insured premises, owned, rented or controlled by the Insured.

As counsel for Frogstar what arguments would you make against coverage?

Problem 105

Bob and Sally Reinhart owned a new motorhome/camper-van. When a panel in the ceiling of the van was opened, the roof extended upward to reveal sleeping quarters. Additionally, a canvas roof extended from the sliding door in the van to make something of a porch from the side of the van. Alone the first evening at their wilderness campsite, Sally cooked dinner over a camp stove just outside the canvas porch while Bob sat cleaning his rifle in a deck chair on the porch.

Questions

1. As dusk grew to dark, Bob spotted what he thought was his first deer of the season about 200 yards away in the underbrush. He pulled his rifle from beside his chair, aimed and fired, instantly maiming Adam Ladue, another camper, who was hiking through the underbrush. Sued by Ladue for negligent discharge of the rifle, Bob has an automobile liability insurance policy for the van which will cover all acts "arising out of the ownership, operation, maintenance, use, loading or unloading of the insured automobile." Bob and Sally also have a homeowners policy which excludes coverage for any act "arising out of the ownership, operation, maintenance, use, loading or unloading of an

automobile." Is Bob insured for the Ladue claim under either of these policies. Who bears the risk of nonpersuasion?

2. Assume instead that after dinner, Bob and Sally rolled up the canvas porch and took a drive. While on that drive, Bob spotted a deer on the side of the road. Grabbing his rifle from the back seat, Bob kept one eye on the road and one on the deer. He fired and severely injured Maryanne Davis, picnicking on the side of the road. Assume the same insurance policies as in Question 1 above.

a. Which of the insurance policies pays if Bob is driving the van?

b. Which of the insurance policies pays if Bob is a passenger and Sally is driving?

3. Assume, in Question 2, that Bob was driving and that as Bob was turning around to grab the rifle, it discharged because Bob had unintentionally left the safety off? Does your answer to the Question of which policy covers change?

4. Assume, in Question 2, that Bob was driving and that, among their belongings in the luggage section of the van, Bob and Sally were carrying a 25 gallon can of highly volatile household cleaner that Sally was afraid to leave at home, because of the extremely hot and dry weather conditions which had existed around their house for several months. Sally figured it would simply be easier to carry the fluid and allow it to be cooled by air conditioning and the wilderness air. As Bob grabbed the rifle, his eyes were distracted by an oncoming car, he mistakenly grabbed the trigger, the gun fired through the lock mechanism of the tailgate of the van, the tailgate opened slightly and the 25

gallon can fell out. When that can was struck by Alex Gates in the next following car, it ignited, causing Gates serious and permanent injuries. Which, if either, of the policies in Question 1 are applicable to this loss?

5. Assume that all went well on their trip and that Bob and Sally returned home from what could only be characterized as a very successful hunting trip. Bob had kept his two guns in a roof top luggage rack. As he stepped on the running board on the side of the van and reached up to the luggage rack, he slipped, grabbed one of the guns by the trigger, the gun discharged, and Doris Leesmont, Bob's next store neighbor, was seriously injured. The homeowners insurer argues that this injury resulted from "loading or unloading of a motor vehicle" and is not covered? What result.

6. Assume that, in Question 5, Bob did unload the gun from the camper and took it into the garage on his way to his gun rack in the basement. In the garage, Bob slipped on motor oil which had leaked out of the van and onto the garage floor. At that point the gun discharged and Mrs. Leesmont was injured. Does your answer change?

PROBLEM 106

Recently, Cal Haddock won a large sum in the state lottery. He decided to fulfill a lifelong ambition and learn to scuba dive. He enrolled in the Salmon Scuba School for a course of six lessons on basic diving. On the first day of classes he met Arthur Skate, his instructor, who made him sit through several boring lectures and videotapes on scuba safety. Haddock complained that this was not what he had in mind. Skate, though dubious of Haddock's ability, finally relented and allowed Haddock to take one shallow practice dive.

Skate drove Haddock to a nearby lake in Salmon's school bus and on the way provided some rudimentary guidance on how to use the scuba equipment.

Haddock donned the equipment which he had purchased and brought with him as Skate started the engine of the Salmon school skiff that was kept moored at the lake. They used the skiff to get to the floating dock that was moored off shore. School policy was to permit only advanced students to dive from the dock. Skate gave Haddock some final instructions about the equipment but did not mention any dangers associated with the lake. Haddock proceeded to dive into the murky depths.

Skate had left the bus engine running so returned to shore. Suddenly, there was a hideous scream from the floating dock. Skate looked up to see Haddock being chased by an alligator. Skate grabbed one of the school's spear guns from its storage bin in the skiff and took a shot at the alligator. He missed badly and jumped onto the hood of the parked school bus to get a better angle. This time he was successful and hit the alligator with a spear. Unfortunately, the spear went through the alligator and hit Haddock causing him severe personal injuries.

Haddock has filed a negligence action against the Salmon Scuba School. During discovery Haddock's attorneys were informed of the following insurance coverages.

First, a liability policy on the floating dock provided by Shoal Mutual which stated:

> We agree to pay on behalf of the insured all sums which the insured shall become legally obligated to pay as damages because of bodily injury or property damage arising out of the ownership, maintenance or use of the floating dock.

Second, a liability policy on the boat written by Mussel Regional Insurance which stated that:

> The insurer agrees to pay on behalf of the insured all sums which the insured shall become legally obligated to pay as damages because of bodily injury or property damage, to which this insurance applies, arising out of the ownership, use, loading or unloading of the insured vessel.

Third, liability coverage on the school bus provided by Dolphin Underwriters Exchange as follows:

> The insurer agrees to pay on behalf of the insured all sums which the insured shall become legally obligated to pay as damages because of bodily injury or property damage, to which this insurance applies, arising out of the ownership, maintenance or use of [the insured vehicle].

Following complete disinterest shown by the insurers in entering into any settlement negotiations, Haddock seeks a declaratory judgement to determine coverage of his accident against all three of the insurers. What result?

Notes

E. FISCHER & P. SWISHER, Principles of Insurance Law, *Estes Co. of Bettendorf v. Employers Mut. Cas. Co.*, p. 386; *Foss v. Cignarella*, p. 394; *Allstate Ins. Co. v. Gillespie*, p. 397; notes & Questions, pp. 398-400 (Matthew Bender, 1986); R. JERRY, Understanding Insurance Law, §§135A; 135B (Matthew Bender, 1987); R. KEETON, Basic Insurance Law, *State Automobile & Casualty Underwriters v. Beeson*, p. 500; *State Farm Mutual Automobile Ins. Co. v. Partridge*, p. 510 (West, 1977); A. WIDISS, Insurance, *Auto-Owners Ins. Co. v. Transamerica Ins. Co.*, p. 817 (West, 1989); K. YORK & J. WHELAN, Insurance Law (Second Edition), *American States Ins. Co. v. Allstate Ins. Co.*, p. 587; notes, pp. 588-592 (West, 1988).

C. Acts Which Are Expected or Intended

Problem 107

Rex was working alone in an all night convenience store. At about 3 a.m., Morrison came into the store apparently to buy some beer. Rex asked him for some identification; an argument developed which escalated into some minor pushing and shoving. At some point Morrison pulled out a knife and told Rex to stay away from him. Rex thought that Morrison was about to attack him and decided to make a preemptive strike. He rushed toward Morrison and knocked him to the ground. Morrison suffered minor stab wounds in the ensuing struggle. In a subsequent criminal proceeding, Morrison pleaded guilty to a charge of second degree assault.

Rex has filed suit against Morrison for assault and battery. His prayer requests $15,000 in compensatory damages.

The relevant insuring clause in Morrison's homeowner's insurance policy with Tupelo Insurance Company has a specific "exclusion" for "conduct expected or intended from the standpoint of the insured."

Tupelo sought a declaratory judgement that it was under no duty to defend or indemnify Morrison. What result? Why?

Problem 108

Gertrude was injured in an automobile accident 6 years ago. She suffered severe injuries in her legs. She was treated for some three years by Dr. Leslie, a specialist in orthopedics. However, she continued to suffer acute pains in her legs and had symptoms of premature osteoarthritis. On a sunny day in June, 2 years ago, Gertrude left her house, apparently to drive to work. In fact she went to the parking lot outside Dr. Leslie's office. When Dr. Leslie drove up Gertrude shot him in the legs with a twelve gauge shotgun. Gertrude then phoned for an ambulance and the police. She was arrested on a charge of assault with intent to maim and sent for psychiatric evaluation at a state facility. Despite prolonged investigations no firm diagnosis was concluded. Court appointed counsel engineered a plea-bargaining agreement whereby Gertrude pleaded guilty to a reduced charge of flourishing a deadly weapon.

Dr. Leslie brought suit against Gertrude on theories of negligence, assault and battery. Whimsical Insurance Co. disputed coverage and requested a declaration of its rights and obligations under Gertrude's homeowner's policy. The insuring clause of that policy stated that Whimsical would "pay all sums the insured must legally pay as damages because of bodily injury or property damage to which this insurance applies." There was a specific exclusion for damages resulting from "assault, battery or felony."

What arguments will Gertrude make? How will the court decide the issues presented?

Problem 109

Billy Guy is a disgruntled former employee of Parliament Explosives Inc. He had been employed in Parliament's plant safety department but was fired for smoking on the job. Billy decided to take revenge on his ex-employer by stealing examples of their new line of super-explosive fireworks and selling them to a rival manufacturer.

Billy had identified the transportation of the fireworks as the major weakness in Parliament's security. Specifically, Billy knew that Harry Fawkes, one of Parliament's drivers, had a habit of pausing on his delivery route at the Westminster Cafe for an unauthorized coffee break.

One morning Billy waited in the parking lot at the cafe until Fawkes showed up. Displaying complete indifference to the security of the dangerous load he was transporting, Fawkes left his truck unlocked and the keys in the ignition. Billy was making good his escape in the truck when a police car pulled into the parking lot. Billy panicked and drove the truck straight at the police car. The driver of the police car swerved out of the way and Billy collided with a traffic signal. The impact caused the truck's fuel tank to explode which in turn set off the fireworks. One firework exploded close to James Royal, a bystander, who sustained serious personal injuries.

James Royal brought suit against Parliament and Billy Guy. Against Parliament he alleged negligence and strict liability with regard to its method of storage and transportation of explosives. Additionally, he alleged Parliament's vicarious liability for the negligence and recklessness of Harry Fawkes. In his complaint against Billy Guy, Royal alleged assault, battery and negligence. Royal seeks compensatory damages of $500,000 and punitive damages in the same amount.

Billy Guy's parents have a homeowner's policy written by the High Risk Insurance Co. Parliament has a general liability policy written by Mutual of Anystate. The High Risk and Mutual Policies contained identical insuring clauses which stated, "We will pay all sums the insured must legally pay as damages because of bodily injury or property damage to which this insurance applies, caused by an accident." The High Risk policy defined "accident" as "conduct neither expected nor intended from the standpoint of the insured." The Mutual policy excluded coverage in the case of "conduct expected or intended from the standpoint of the insured." Limits under each policy were $1 million.

Questions

1. Both insurers now seek a declaratory judgment that its policy is not liable for this loss. Discuss.

2. If testimony revealed that Billy Guy was a diabetic and was suffering an acute hyperglycemic attack at the time, would your answer be different? How?

3. Assume that James Royal was granted leave to amend his petition to allege negligent supervision of Billy Guy by his parents. Does your answer change? How?

PROBLEM 110

Willard and Stanley were septuagenarian neighbors living in a trailer park. They had been friends and drinking buddies for twenty years. One night, in the middle of a game of poker, Stanley started shouting at Willard and, apparently without provocation, reached for his shotgun, and discharged it, killing Willard. A subsequent blood test showed that Stanley's blood alcohol level was three times that used as the legal definition for drunk driving. Subsequent to the killing, Stanley suffered total memory loss and was institutionalized for treatment of acute alcoholism.

Stanley was the named insured under a homeowner's policy with the plaintiff. The Allrisk policy excluded coverage for "bodily injury or property damage which is expected or intended by the insured."

Allrisk investigated the matter, filed an action for declaratory judgment and, at trial, moved for a directed verdict. What result? Why?

Notes

E. FISCHER & P. SWISHER, Principles of Insurance Law, Meaning of "Expected" or "Intended", p. 402; *Safeco Ins. Co. of America v. Dotts*, p. 402; notes & Questions, p. 405 (Matthew Bender, 1986); R. HENDERSON, Insurance Law, *Argonaut Southwest Ins. Co. v. Maupin*, p. 174; *Millard Warehouse, Inc. v. Hartford Fire Ins. Co.*, p. 177; notes, pp. 187-190; *Farmers Ins. Group v. Sessions*, p. 190; notes, pp. 194-97; *Transamerica Ins. Group v. Meere*, p. 197; notes, p. 206 (Michie, 1989); R. JERRY, Understanding Insurance Law, §63B (Matthew Bender, 1987); R. KEETON & A. WIDISS, Insurance Law, §§5.4(a); (b)(1), (2), (4); (c)(1)-(7); (e) (West, 1988); R. KEETON, Basic Insurance Law, *Argonaut Southwest Ins. Co. v. Maupin*, p. 449; *Big Town Nursing Homes, Inc. v. Reserve Ins. Co.*, p. 453; *State Farm Fire & Casualty Co. v. Muth*, p. 456; *Hartford Fire Ins. Co. v. Wagner*, p. 461; *Pawtucket Mutual Ins. Co. v. Lebrecht*, p. 463; *Fox Wisconsin Corp. v. Century Indemnity Co.*, p. 465; *Hartford Accident & Indemnity Co. v. Wolbarst*, p. 466 (West, 1977); A. WIDISS, Insurance, *Ambassador Ins. Co. v. Montes*, p. 333; Liability Insurance for Intentional Torts; p. 496; *Brown v. State Automobile*, p. 498; Insurance Coverage for "Highly Expectable" Losses, p. 503; *Gray v. Zurich Ins. Co.*, p. 805, 807; *Marilyn Casualty Co. v. Peppers*, p. 821 (West, 1989); K. YORK & J. WHELAN, Insurance Law (Second Edition), *Pachucki v. Republic Ins. Co.*, p. 537; notes, pp. 543-45 (West, 1988); W. YOUNG & E. HOLMES, Insurance, Expectable Claims for Property Loss or Damage, p. 250; notes, pp. 252-53; *Farmers Ins. Co. of Arizona v. Vagnozzi*, p. 253; notes, pp. 256-57; Child Molestation, p. 257; *MacKinnon v. Hanover Ins. Co.*, p. 258; notes, p. 260; *Ambassador Ins. Co. v. Montes*, p. 261; notes, pp. 268-69 (Foundation, 1985).

D. Other Insurance Clauses

Problem 111

The underlying action involves a wrongful death claim by the survivors of a patient against a hospital alleging medical malpractice. Having reserved their rights with respect to the issues that follow, the insurers settled the claim for $1 million.

The hospital had acquired $1 million coverage from Best Insurance in

1984. The insuring clause stated, "we will pay amounts the hospital is legally obligated to pay to compensate others for injury resulting from providing or failing to provide professional services . . ." Additionally, the Best policy contained the following clause:

> If an insured has other insurance for a loss covered by this policy, the insurance afforded under this policy shall be excess over any other valid and collectible insurance.

The hospital administrator was worried that the Best policy would not cover wrongful death claims and, in 1986, he purchased coverage of $2 million from Grand Mutual. The salient portions of the Grand Mutual policy read as follows:

> We will pay amounts the hospital is legally obligated to pay to compensate others for injury or death resulting from providing or failing to provide professional services . . .
>
> * * *
>
> A professional liability loss that's covered under this agreement may also be covered under other insurance. If this happens, we'll pay that portion of the loss which the limits of coverage under the agreement are of the total of all limits that apply. But we won't pay more than the limits of coverage under this agreement.

Grand Mutual brought an action against Best seeking declaration of rights under the policies. The federal district court entered summary judgment in favor of Best on the following issues:

1. No Question of conflicting "other insurance" clauses or apportionment thereof could arise unless each insurer could have been liable ultimately for the same loss. The Best policy involved no such exposure.

2. The *Lamb-Weston* approach to overlapping "other insurance" clauses

is fundamentally flawed because it replaces traditional rules of contractual interpretation with mechanistic judicial regulation which has no basis in law.

3. In any event, the particular clauses here in issue are not mutually repugnant, but may be reconciled using traditional interpretative methodologies.

4. In the event that an appellate court should consider that some form of extra-contractual allocation is proper, such reallocation should be performed on the basis of equal shares between the insurers. Thus, both Best and Grand Mutual each would be responsible for $500,000.

Discuss.

Problem 112

Mary Allison had her automobile brakes repaired at BRAKO, a local repair shop. When she drove out of the shop, she received BRAKO's "Insurance Guaranty" which provided that BRAKO would replace the brakes if, "within 45 days, the brakes fail because of any error in workmanship or installation by BRAKO." The next day, while driving her car at 65 miles per hour in a 35 mph zone, Mary failed to see a Stop sign, proceeded through it, and collided with Jackson Davey's car. Mary claims that she saw the Davey car at the last instant, but when she attempted to slam on her brakes, they failed. Mary has automobile insurance with Allrisk. Her policy provides, among other things, for "Other Insurance:"

> Where there is other applicable insurance against a loss covered by this policy, the Company shall not be liable under this policy for a greater proportion of such loss than the applicable limit of liability stated in the declarations bears to the total applicable limit of liability of all valid and collectable insurance

against such loss.

Independent investigation has confirmed that the brakes on Mary's car failed because of a defect in workmanship by BRAKO and, as a result, Allrisk seeks to be liable for only a proportionate share of the liability. What result? Why?

PROBLEM 113

This problem is based on the facts in *Residents of Eldon Beach v. Blissful, J.D. Excavating Co., and Waste Management Corp.*, Problem 99. Assume that the court held the prior insurance for each of the defendants applicable to the facts of the case and that each such insurer agreed to defend. Each of the three insurance policies has a policy limit of $500,000. The total damages flowing from the spread of the toxic dirt is $950,000.

The Blissful policy provides, under the language "Other Insurance," as follows:

> This Insurance Policy shall not be liable to make any payment in connection with any claim made against an insured which claim is insured by any other valid insurance policy.

The J.D. Excavating Co. policy provides, under the language "Other Insurance," as follows:

> If there is any other valid and collectible insurance which would apply in the absence of this policy, the insurance under this policy shall apply only as excess insurance over such other insurance.

The Waste Management Corporations policy provides, under the language "Other Insurance," as follows:

> If there is any other insurance against a loss covered by this policy, this Company shall not be liable under this policy for a greater proportion of such loss than the applicable limit of

liability stated in the declarations bears to the total applicable limit of liability of all valid and collectible insurance against such loss.

Assume that the Court would like to give effect to each of these "Other Insurance" clauses.

Questions

1. If the court simply enforces the clauses as written, how will the $950,000 loss be paid?

2. If the court employs the *Lamb-Weston* rule, how will the $950,000 be paid? Is this a proper case for use of *Lamb-Weston*?

3. If the court employs a primary-secondary analysis, how will the $950,000 be paid?

Problem 114

This problem is based on Question 4 in the problem of *Alex Gates v. Bob and Sally Reinhart*, Problem 105. Assume that the Automobile Insurer agreed from the outset to defend the lawsuit, and that the Homeowners Insurer later entered into defense. The lawyer hired by the Automobile carrier continued to defend the Insured, and tried the case to a conclusion. Both the Automobile Insurance and Homeowners Insurance have pro rata "Other Insurance" clauses. Can the Automobile Insurance Co. expect contribution from the Homeowners Insurance Co. for all or part of the litigation expenses incurred by the Automobile Insurance Co.? Assume that the court determines that one of the insurers is to be primary and one is to be secondary. Will this change your answer? How will the court make the primary/secondary decision?

Notes

E. FISCHER & P. SWISHER, Principles of Insurance Law, What is "Other Insurance", p. 571; *Liberty Mutual Ins. Co. v. Home Ins. Co.*, p. 572; *Georgia Casualty & Surety Co. v. Universal Underwriters Ins. Co.*, p. 577; *Sloviaczek v. Estate of Puckett*, p. 579; notes & Questions, pp. 583-84; *American Star Ins. Co. v. Allstate Ins. Co.*, p. 584 (Matthew Bender, 1986); R. HENDERSON, Insurance Law, *Carriers Ins. Co. v. American Policyholders Ins. Co.*, p. 118; notes, pp. 123-25 (Michie, 1989); R. JERRY, Understanding Insurance Law, §97 (Matthew Bender, 1987); R. KEETON & A. WIDISS, Insurance Law, §3.11 (West, 1988); R. KEETON, Basic Insurance Law, *Werley v. United Services Automobile Ass'n.*, p. 255; *Hardware Dealers Mutual Fire Ins. Co. v. Farmers Ins. Exchange*, p. 263 (West, 1977); A. WIDISS, Insurance, Other Insurance Clauses, p. 230; *Jones v. Medox*, p. 232; *Mission Insurance Co. v. Allendale Mut. Ins. Co.*, p. 240; *Mission Insurance Co. v. United States Fire Ins. Co.*, p. 243 (West, 1989); K. YORK & J. WHELAN, Insurance Law, Preliminary Note, pp. 681-83; *Jones v. Medox, Inc.*, p. 683; *Carriers Ins. Co. v. American Policyholders Ins. Co.*, p. 689; *Continental Casualty Co. v. Reserve Ins. Co.*, p. 695 (Second Edition) (West, 1988); W. YOUNG & E. HOLMES, Insurance, The Riddle of "Other Insurance," p. 137 (Foundation, 1985).

E. Liability Insurance for Special Classes

1. *Insureds with Sovereign or Charitable Immunity*

Problem 115

Good Neighbor Insurance provides property insurance for a large number of nursing homes situated in the southern United States. Many of these enjoy charitable immunity under applicable state tort doctrine. Good Neighbor now wishes to market its premises and professional liability coverages to this important client base.

We have been asked to assist Good Neighbor by supplying rationales for the purchase of such coverages by their immune clients. Additionally, we have been requested to identify any specific clauses that we would recommend including in a liability policy in this type of situation. Please identify any such clauses and whether their use is susceptible to successful challenge.

Problem 116

As indicated in the preceding problem, Good Neighbor Insurance already sells property insurance to nursing homes. Many of them are really State, County, City elderly care facilities, which are wholly owned and operated by the government owner. As a result, they enjoy sovereign immunity under applicable state tort doctrine. Good Neighbor wishes to market its premises and professional liability coverages to this important client base.

We have been asked to assist Good Neighbor by supplying rationales for the purchase of such coverages by their immune clients. Additionally, we have been requested to identify any specific clauses that we would recommend including in a liability policy in this type of situation. Please identify any such clauses and whether their use is susceptible to successful challenge.

Notes

R. JERRY, Understanding Insurance Law, §95[d] (Matthew Bender, 1987); R. KEETON & A. WIDISS, Insurance Law, §4.8(d) (West, 1988); R. KEETON, Basic Insurance Law, *Koenig v. Milwaukee Blood Center, Inc.*, p. 356; *Michael v. St. Paul Mercury Indemnity Co.*, p. 358; *Pohland v. City of Sheboygan*, p. 359.

2. *Professional Insureds*

Problem 117

Five years ago, Wanda Swift set up her law practice in a small town near yours. Wanda did mostly personal injury plaintiff's work and was immediately successful. When she first started, she purchased malpractice insurance coverage from Allied Casualty Co. One of Wanda's early clients was Alfred Draper who was injured while riding in a car being driven by a friend of his, Mickey Hatch. Mickey had picked Alfred up on a very cold morning and, when he got in, Alfred could just barely see out the window, as Mickey had scrapped off just two small holes in the windshield. On the way to work, Mickey's car had a blow-out but Mickey was able to steer the car onto the shoulder on the opposite side of the street where Mickey stopped. Just as Alfred was about to get out, Mickey's car was struck at the passenger side rear bumper by a truck being driven by Martin Richards. As it turned out, Mickey had not pulled all the way off the road and not been able to see the Richards' truck as it approached. Alfred suffered severe injuries and hired Wanda to represent him in a lawsuit telling Wanda that he did not want to see Mickey harmed. Wanda filed suit against Richards alone. At trial of that suit which was held one year ago, Richards continued to allege that the accident was mostly Mickey's fault in not cleaning off the window and not pulling all the way off the road. The jury assessed the liability of Richards at 15%, and found that Alfred's total damages amounted to $150,000. As a result, Alfred received a judgment for $22,500, of which Wanda took $7,500. In addition, filing fees of the lawsuit, depositions, and expert medical witnesses cost another $2,500 with the result that Alfred actually received $12,500 for all of his injuries.

Dissatisfied with this result, Alfred has now filed suit against Wanda

Swift alleging that she was negligent in failing to join Mickey Hatch as a defendant to the lawsuit.

Questions

1. Assume that the malpractice policy which Wanda purchased from Allied Casualty Co. five years ago provided, in part for the following coverage:

> This insurance will pay on behalf of the Insured all sums which the Insured shall become legally obligated to pay as damages because of any claim or claims made against the Insured during the policy period arising out of the performance of professional services by any person for whose acts or omissions the Insured partnership, corporation, or professional association is legally responsible.

This policy was terminated when Allied went out of the malpractice insurance business 3 years ago. As a result, Wanda purchased another policy from First Vernon Insurance Company. That policy provided, in part:

> This insurance will pay on behalf of the Insured all sums which the Insured shall become legally obligated to pay as a result of an occurrence during the policy period arising out of the performance of professional services by any person for whose acts or omissions the Insured partnership, corporation, or professional association is legally responsible.

When sued by Alfred, which Company will pick up coverage for Wanda and pay the claim?

2. Assume that Wanda's two malpractice insurance policies were purchased in just the reverse order from in Question 1. Which of the two policies will pick up the coverage for Wanda and pay the claim?

3. Assume, in Question 2, that when Wanda purchased the second, "claims made" policy, it provided as follows:

> THIS IS A CLAIMS MADE POLICY--It covers all claims relating to the insured's performance of professional services arising subsequent to the retroactive date stated on the Declarations page.

On the Declarations page were two dates: "Effective Date--November 1, 3 years ago" and "Retroactive Date--November 1, 3 years ago." November 1 is the date that Wanda purchased the policy. How does this clause affect your answer to Question 2? Are there any public policy difficulties with the clause?

4. Assume that when Allied Casualty Ins. Co. went out of the malpractice business, it was able to offer limited "continuation protection" to its former insureds. That coverage provided as follows:

> For an additional premium to be computed at the Company's then existing rules, rates, rating plans and premiums applicable on the effective date of this endorsement, the Insured shall have an endorsement providing additional Reporting Periods in which claims otherwise covered by this policy may be reported.

Under which of the two scenarios, that in Question 1 or that in Question 2 is Wanda more likely to want to purchase this endorsement?

Problem 118

Gabriel O'Mallett, a newly admitted lawyer, engaged in permitted lawyer advertising in which he listed his name under a telephone directory banner of "Lawyers by Field of Practice." Anthony Gilbert saw Gabriel's name under the listing for "Wills and Trusts" and sought Gabriel's help for planning and preparation of a unique personal trust for Anthony Gilbert. In fact, Gabriel had never prepared either a Will or a Trust, and had done poorly in the course in law school. His advertising in the field of practice section was done by him to get the widest exposure possible, and without any regard for the categories in which he was advertising. After the trust was severely penalized under federal tax laws for failing to include a trust provision which any competent trust lawyer would have included, Gilbert hired a new lawyer and filed suit against Gabriel. Suit was filed under the state deceptive trade practice act, which applies to services, and which provides a treble damage remedy to persons who are victimized by deceptive advertising. Gabriel had a malpractice policy which provided "claims made coverage" with the following exclusion:

> This insurance does not apply to any dishonest, fraudulent, criminal or malicious act or omission.

When it received the claim filed by Gilbert, Gabriel's insurer refused to defend the claim alleging that it arose from "dishonest" conduct, alleging that the conduct would violate the applicable code of professional conduct for lawyers. What result?

Problem 119

Ralph Shoemaker had been an insurance agent for most of his life. Shoemaker was the exclusive local agent for Province Casualty Co., a national leader in Products Liability Insurance. Five years ago, he sold "products liability" insurance to Cape Products, Inc., which manufactured control "boards" for personal computers. Unbeknownst to Shoemaker, the policy did not cover losses sustained by a computer user to an individual computer program itself or losses resulting from the down-time of the computer. The policy did cover any damages to the "board" itself. Two years ago, Cape Products, Inc. was sued by Florence Spatz, damaged when a Cape Products "board" shorted out, caused electrical shock to Florence, burned out her computer and caused her to miss a deadline on a major new book she was preparing. The latter resulted in Florence's failure to be the first into a major new market. Florence claimed damages for $25,000 for personal injuries; $4,000 for property damage to the computer; and $250,000 in lost royalties from the book. Province Casualty has agreed to defend and pay the Personal Injury and Property Damage claim, but refuses to defend the lost royalties. When Cape Products received this news, it wrote to Ralph Shoemaker and indicated that Cape Products was "disappointed that these losses might not be covered. We thought that all of our potential liability would be covered by this policy, however, it looks like there was a miscommunication between us somewhere." Ralph heard nothing about the matter for 2 years after this letter (although he was not asked to write more insurance for Cape Products). Last week, however, Ralph was sued for the lost royalties which Cape Products, Inc. was obligated to pay to Florence Spatz. Concerned with a rising tide of insurance agent/broker malpractice claims, last year, Ralph purchased his own professional "claims made" liability policy. Claim is defined as "the assertion of a legal right through a demand for money or services." Ralph immediately sent his suit papers to his company, however the company called yesterday and advised that a "claim" was made before the effective date of the policy and is, therefore, outside the coverage. Discuss.

Notes

R. HENDERSON, Insurance Law, *Continental Casualty Co. v. Burton*, p. 293; notes, pp. 299-301; *Continental Copper & Steel Ind. v. Johnson*, p. 301; note, p. 306 (Michie, 1989); R. KEETON & A. WIDISS, Insurance Law, §§5.4(d)(8), 5.10(d) (West, 1988); R. KEETON, Basic Insurance Law, *Big Town Nursing Homes, Inc. v. Reserve Ins. Co.*, p. 453; *Gyler v. Mission Ins. Co.*, p. 571 (West, 1977); A. WIDISS, Insurance, "Claims Made" Coverage, p. 576; *Sparks v. St. Paul Ins. Co.*, p. 624 (West, 1989); K. YORK & J. WHELAN, Insurance Law (Second Edition), *New England Reinsurance Corporation v. National Union Fire Ins. Co. of Pittsburgh*, p. 528 (West, 1988); W. YOUNG & E. HOLMES, Insurance, *Perl v. St. Paul Fire & Marine Ins. Co.*, p. 103; *Public Service Mut. Ins. Co. v. Goldfarb*, p. 306 (Foundation, 1985).

Chapter Eight

Automobile Insurance

A. Coverage Issues

1. "*Owned and Non-Owned Automobiles*"

Problem 120

Ernest Reardon had owned two automobiles, a 4 year old Ford and a 2 year old Chevrolet. Last April, he called the agent for First State Insurance, which carried the automobile insurance on both cars, and had the 4 year old Ford removed from the policy. To replace that car, Reardon, as President of Razorback Construction Co, Inc., a corporation which Reardon formed and for which he was the sole shareholder, purchased a brand new pick-up truck. That truck, according to the corporate minutes of Razorback Construction Co., Inc., was assigned to President Reardon for his regular use. Reardon had an accident with the truck, has been sued by the victims of that accident, and has turned the claim over to First State. The policy Reardon has with First State provides, in part:

> INSUREDS: As used in this policy, "Insured" or "Insureds" refers to the named insured with respect to the owned or a non-owned automobile provided the use of such non-owned automobile is with the permission, or reasonably believed to be with the permission of the owner and is within the scope of such permission.
>
> * * *
>
> NON-OWNED AUTOMOBILE: "Non-owned automobile" means a land motor vehicle designed for use principally upon public roads which is not owned by, or furnished or available for the regular use of the named insured or any resident of the household of the named insured other than a temporary substitute automobile.

First State has refused defense of the claim on behalf of Reardon. Is First State correct in this refusal? If the vehicle is neither owned nor non-owned, what is it?

PROBLEM 121

Marcia Peace was an engineer with TransPacific Electric, a major, publicly owned utility. As part of her job, Marcia, as did other members of the engineering department, had to go into the field and make inspections of electric transmission lines. TransPacific owned 12 automobiles which its various employees had to check out to use on company business. The practice was for the employee, such as Marcia, to go to the auto pool, request and then obtain a company vehicle. In actuality, Marcia was on the road 4-5 days a week and, as a result, she used one particular Bronco on 1-2 of those days and a Chevy Blazer on the remainder of the days. On the day in question, Marcia, together with two other TransPacific engineers, went to the auto pool and requested a vehicle so the three of them could jointly inspect some transmission lines. By mere happenstance, the first keys available were those of the Ford Bronco and they were thrown to Marcia who drove the vehicle. Marcia went off the road, injuring the other two engineers. Marcia is personally insured for her own automobile by the Atlantic Insurance Company, by an automobile policy which insures Marcia while driving either an "owned" or a "non-owned" automobile. The policy defines "non-owned" automobile as follows:

> "Non-owned automobile" means a land motor vehicle designed for use principally upon public roads which is not owned by, or furnished or available for the regular use of the named insured or any resident of the household of the named insured other than a temporary substitute automobile, provided such use is with the permission, or reasonably believed to be with the permission of the owner and is within the scope of such permission.

The Atlantic Insurance Company refuses to defend Marcia in the action against her by the injured engineers. What result? Why?

PROBLEM 122

Paulene McBride owned her own car and had it insured with Commerce National Insurance Company. Paulene lived at home with her mother and father, who owned their own car. While Paulene's car was in the shop being repaired, she borrowed her father's car, with his permission, to go back and forth to work. While coming home from work, Paulene caused an accident and is being sued by two injured persons. Paulene's policy with Commerce provides coverage for Paulene whether she is driving an "owned" or "non-owned" automobile. The policy then provides:

> "Non-owned automobile" means a land motor vehicle designed for use principally upon public roads which is not owned by, or furnished or available for the regular use of the named insured or any resident of the household of the named insured other than a temporary substitute automobile.
>
> * * *
>
> "Temporary Substitute Automobile" means an automobile not owned by the named insured or any resident of the same household, while temporarily used with the permission of the owner, as a substitute for the described automobile when withdrawn from normal use because of its breakdown, repair, servicing, loss or destruction.

Questions

1. Commerce National Insurance Co. has refused to defend Paulene against the suits filed against Paulene. Is this refusal correct?

2. Suppose when she purchased the insurance, Paulene had asked her agent, "How am I covered when I am not driving my own car?" and the agent said: "You're covered whenever you are driving either your own car or any non-owned car." What arguments can you make for coverage in this case?

Notes

E. FISCHER & P. SWISHER, Principles of Insurance Law, *Kelly v. Aetna Casualty & Surety Co.*, p. 346; *Simon v. Lumbermens Mutual Casualty Co.*, p. 349; notes & questions, pp. 350-51 (Matthew Bender, 1986); R. HENDERSON, Insurance Law, *Farmers Ins. Co. v. USF&G Co.*, p. 462 (Michie, 1989); R. JERRY, Understanding Insurance Law, §135B (Matthew Bender, 1987); R. KEETON & A. WIDISS,

Insurance Law, §4.9(b)(c) (West, 1988); A. WIDISS, Insurance, The Marketing of Standard Insurance Contracts, pp. 101-102; 106-117 (West, 1989).

2. *"Use Of" or "Operation" of an "Automobile"*

PROBLEM 123

Ben Whitehead met his friend, and deputy county sheriff Gordon Galemore at a basketball game. After the game, when Ben and Gordon went out into the parking lot, they found a man known to Galemore as Jerome Elmore smashing the windshield of Whitehead's car. Galemore quickly placed Elmore under arrest and escorted Elmore to the back seat of Galemore's car. Because his car was damaged, Whitehead decided to ride home with Galemore. Shortly after Galemore started his car, Elmore drew a pistol from his pocket and threatened Galemore. Galemore quickly drew a pistol he kept under the seat and shots were fired. Galemore stopped the car as more shots were being fired, Elmore and Galemore both jumped out, and eventually Elmore was recaptured and disarmed. Whitehead, however, was wounded by the gunfire. Galemore has an automobile insurance policy which pays medical expenses to persons who suffer injuries while "using" Galemore's motor vehicle. Will Galemore's insurer be obligated to pay Whitehead's medical expenses?

PROBLEM 124

Last Thursday, Paula Reeves's car broke down on a deserted stretch of County Road. Unable to fix the car herself, Paula began to walk in an effort to find aid. About two miles from where she had left her car, while she was still walking and trying to find help in repairing her car, Paula was struck by another vehicle. Paula suffered numerous injuries. Paula has a standard automobile insurance policy which includes medical expense coverage. Are her injuries covered?

Problem 125

While walking his dog, Robert Havens was struck by a car which rolled out of the driveway of James Sampson's house. Sampson's 3 year old son had gotten into the car, disengaged the brake of the manual transmission car, and the vehicle rolled down the driveway into Havens. The car was covered by Sampson's automobile policy which provided coverage to any member of Sampson's household while "using" the motor vehicle. Are the actions by Sampson and his son covered by this policy?

Notes

E. FISCHER & P. SWISHER, Principles of Insurance Law, Exclusionary Clauses, p. 357; "Arising Out Of," p. 357; *Auto-Owners Ins. Co. v. Transamerica Ins. Co.*, p. 358; notes & questions, p. 360; *Foss v. Cignarella*, p. 394; *Allstate Ins. Co. v. Gillespie*, p. 397; notes & questions, pp. 398-400 (Matthew Bender, 1986); R. HENDERSON, Insurance Law, *McNeill v. Maryland Ins. Guaranty Ass'n.*, p. 264; notes, pp. 268-270 (Michie, 1989); R. JERRY, Understanding Insurance Law, §135B (Matthew Bender, 1987); R. KEETON & A. WIDISS, Insurance Law, §5.2(b) (West, 1988); R. KEETON, Basic Insurance Law, *Lukaszewicz v. Concrete Research, Inc.*, p. 346 (West, 1977); A. WIDISS, Insurance, *Allstate Ins. Co. v. Gillespie*, p. 416; *Foss v. Cignarella*, p. 418 (West, 1989); K. YORK & J. WHELAN, Insurance Law (Second Edition), *American States Ins. Co. v. Allstate Ins. Co.*, p. 587; notes, pp. 588-592 (West, 1988).

Problem 126

Sarah Hardy was seriously injured when her friend Daniel Ross negligently drove into a tree while the two of them were driving together. Daniel Ross has an automobile insurance policy which provides coverage to Daniel while he is driving any "Automobile." The policy defines "automobile" as "a land motor vehicle designed for use principally upon public roads." Additionally, state statute requires liability insurance for any "Motor Vehicle." The statute defines "motor vehicle" as "a self-propelled vehicle which is designed for use upon a highway, including trailers designed for use with such vehicles." Sarah has now sued Daniel for her injuries.

Questions

1. Assume that Daniel was driving, and Sarah was riding on a moped and that the accident occurred while the two were driving off-road. Is Daniel covered?

2. Assume that Daniel was driving, and Sarah was riding on a dune-buggy, which Daniel had built himself, which had no closed passenger compartment, but which had passed state motor vehicle safety inspection. Is Daniel covered?

3. Assume that Daniel was driving, and Sarah was riding on a snow-mobile, which was being used by the two of them on a public street which had become clogged with snow to get Sarah to work at a local hospital. Is Daniel covered?

Notes

R. KEETON & A. WIDISS, Insurance Law, §§4.9(b), 4.10(d) (West, 1988); R. KEETON, Basic Insurance Law, A Study in Standardization, pp. 117-19; *Lukaszewicz v. Concrete Research, Inc.*, p. 346 (West, 1977); K. YORK & J. WHELAN, Insurance Law (Second Edition), Automobile Insurance, pp. 17-20 (West, 1988).

B. The Household Exclusion

Problem 127

While driving to their vacation, Mark Adams, his wife Abbie, and their two children, John and Karen, were involved in a motor vehicle accident when Mark ran a red light. Abbie, John, and Karen were all seriously injured in the accident. Mark has the car he was driving insured with All Risks Insurance Co. The policy, however, has an exclusion which provides:

> This policy does not apply under part I [LIABILITY] to the liability of the insured for bodily injury to the named insured or any relative of the named insured who is a resident of the same household.

Questions

1. Are there public policy reasons why this exclusion should or should not be enforced?

2. How do such clauses comport with state mandatory automobile insurance against liability statutes?

3. Assume that Karen Adams was 19 years old, had been fully emancipated by her parents, was only on the trip for old times sake, had already rented her own apartment, and was planning on moving her things out of her

parents' home as soon as the family returned? Is she entitled to recover under the policy?

4. Assume that John Adams was 14 years old, had been in trouble for a long time, had been sent to his grandparents home to live, and had, in fact lived with his grandparents in another city for the 9 months preceding the trip. John was only on the trip for the purpose of trying to effectuate a reconciliation with his parents. The accident took place on the next to last day of the family's planned 2 week trip. Is John entitled to recover under the policy?

5. Assume that Mark and Abbie Adams were never married but have simply lived together and held themselves out as husband and wife for many years. Does this affect Abbie's claim? Karen's?

6. Are Mark, Karen, John, and Abbie barred, by the household exclusion, from all recovery under Mark's automobile policy as a result of the accident? For what can they recover?

Notes

R. HENDERSON, Insurance Law, *Meyer v. State Farm Mut. Automobile Ins. Co.*, p. 466; notes, pp. 473-74 (Michie, 1989); R. JERRY, Understanding Insurance Law, §135C (Matthew Bender, 1987); R. KEETON & A. WIDISS, Insurance Law, §4.9(c)(1) (West, 1988); R. KEETON, Basic Insurance Law, *Salas v. Liberty Mutual Fire Ins. Co.*, p. 359 (West, 1977); A. WIDISS, Insurance, Introductory Notes, pp. 344-47; *State Farm Mut. Ins. Co. v. Sivey*, p. 347; *Florida Farm Bureau Ins. Co. v. Government Employers Ins. Co.*, p. 350; *Sturiano v. Brooks*, p. 352; *Mutual of Enumclaw Ins. Co. v. Wiscomb*, p. 663 (West, 1989); K. YORK & J. WHELAN, Insurance Law (Second Edition), *Farmers Ins. Exchange v. Cocking*, p. 609; notes, 612-14 (West, 1988); W. YOUNG & E. HOLMES, Insurance, *Mutual of Enumclaw Ins. Co. v. Wiscomb*, p. 91; notes, pp. 95-96 (Foundation, 1985).

C. Omnibus Clause

1. Initial Permittees

Problem 128

Randy Rudolph owns a pizza parlor and employs local high school and college age students to deliver pizza to customers in three cars owned by Rudolph. Those cars are all covered by an automobile insurance policy in Rudolph's name, which insures each of the three cars and names as "Insureds:"

> Any other person while using any motor vehicle covered by this policy provided the operation and the actual use of such vehicle are with the permission of the named insured and are within the scope of such permission.

Rudolph has instructed all of his drivers that they are to make their deliveries "by the most direct route possible." He has also advised them that they are not to pick up any passengers. Rudolph knows, however, that his drivers regularly give rides to their friends and Rudolph has not objected so long as the ride does not delay delivery of the pizza.

Questions

1. Zack James is one of Rudolph's regular drivers. James leaves the pizza parlor on his way to a delivery across town. On the way, Zack spots his girlfriend who is walking home from cheerleading practice. After picking her up, but while still on the direct route, James' negligence causes a collision. Will the liability of James be covered by the Rudolph insurance policy?

2. Assume that after James picked up his girlfriend, he deviated from the most direct route to his delivery and tried to take his girlfriend, who lived 5 blocks from the most direct route, home. While on this detour, James' negligence causes a collision. Will the liability of James be covered by the

Rudolph insurance policy?

3. Assume that James picked up his girlfriend and totally forgot about the delivery. He and his girlfriend left for a rock concert in a city 45 miles away. After going to the concert, James' negligent driving causes a collision. Will the liability of James be covered by the Rudolph insurance policy?

Problem 129

Home from work after a particularly hectic day, Marilyn Estes left her car in her driveway and went inside. Unfortunately, Marilyn forgot her car keys. Seeing the keys in the ignition, David, then age 16, hopped into the car, started it up and sped off, shortly thereafter causing an accident. David has no automobile insurance. Marilyn's car is covered by an automobile policy which defines as "Insured:"

> Any other person while using the covered auto provided such use is expressly or impliedly with the permission of the named insured.

Questions

1. Assume that David is Marilyn's son, and that Marilyn had been teaching David how to drive by taking him out on driving sessions, usually just after Marilyn arrived home. Is David's negligence covered by Marilyn's policy?

2. Assume that David is a total stranger who simply stole the vehicle because the keys were left in it. What arguments can be made for providing coverage under Marilyn's policy?

Problem 130

Rudy Teel was thinking of buying a new car and when his friend Davis Mate indicated that Davis was going to sell his car, Rudy was interested. Rudy told Davis that Rudy had to take a business trip for a "few" days and that if Rudy could use Davis' car, Rudy would decide if he wanted to purchase the car. Davis told Rudy: "O.K., but I don't want this to drag on too long. I would like to either have my car back or your money within 3 days." Rudy indicated that he would try to accommodate Davis and Davis thereafter gave Rudy the keys. Six days later, when Rudy had not returned, Davis called the local police and reported the car stolen. Rudy's negligence caused an accident the next day as Rudy was returning from the business trip. The car was insured by Davis with an automobile policy which defined "insured" as "any other person while using the insured vehicle provided that any such use is with the permission of the named insured." When Rudy turned over the suit papers resulting from his accident to Davis' insurer, the company refused defense indicating that permission to Rudy had either expired or been withdrawn. What result?

Notes

E. FISCHER & P. SWISHER, Principles of Insurance Law, *First National Bank v. Aetna Cas. & Sur. Co.*, p. 380; notes & questions, pp. 385-86 (Matthew Bender, 1986); R. HENDERSON, Insurance Law, *Odolecki v. Hartford Acc. & Ind. Co.*, p. 450; notes, p. 454 (Michie, 1989); R. JERRY, Understanding Insurance Law, §51[b] (Matthew Bender, 1987); R. KEETON & A. WIDISS, Insurance Law, §§4.7(a), (b)(1), (3), & (4) (West, 1988); R. KEETON, Basic Insurance Law, *Odolecki v. Hartford Accident & Indemnity Co.*, p. 338; *MacBey v. Hartford Accident & Indemnity Co.*, p. 352; *Bachman v. Independence Indemnity Co.*, p. 354; *Cain v. American Policyholders' Ins. Co.*, p. 354 (West, 1977); A. WIDISS, Insurance, Identifying the Insureds in Casualty Insurance, p. 268; Omnibus Clauses & Coverages, p. 315; *MFA Insurance Companies v. Mendenhall*, p. 316 (West, 1989); K. YORK & J. WHELAN, Insurance Law (Second Edition), *Metz v. Universal Underwriters Ins. Co.*, p. 21; note (and Statutes), pp. 594-96; *Milbank Mutual Ins. Co. v. United States Fidelity and Guaranty Co.*, p. 601; note (and Statutes), pp. 606-608 (West, 1988); W. YOUNG & E. HOLMES, Insurance, *Ryan v. Western Pacific Ins. Co.*, p. 344; notes, p. 349

(Foundation, 1985).

2. *Subsequent Permittees*

Problem 131

Randy Meyer owned an automobile. When approached by his friend Dave about using Randy's car for an important business engagement, Randy said: "Dave, you can use my car at any time. But, if Bob is going with you, and I know Bob is your partner and usually goes with you, I do not want Bob to drive my car under any circumstances. He has had three tickets and I simply do not trust him." Dave readily agreed and left with Randy's car. In fact, Dave did take Bob and go on the business trip. On the way home, Dave became ill and Dave and Bob had to stop in a rest area in the middle of nowhere. It was late at night, there was no help in sight and Bob said: "Davie, I know that Randy doesn't want me to drive, but you can't and we can't wait here forever. What if you are seriously ill?" Reluctantly, Dave agreed. Bob drove from the rest area, across the highway median and crashed into an oncoming auto, causing serious injury. Bob, being without insurance because of his ticket experiences, has turned the resulting suit papers over to Randy.

Questions

1. Assume that Randy's insurance policy defines "insureds" as:

   Any person while operating the automobile provided the actual operation of the automobile is with the permission of the named insured.

Will Randy's policy cover Bob in this circumstance? Why or why not?

2. Assume instead that Randy's insurance policy defines "insureds" as:

> Any person while using the automobile provided the actual use of the automobile is with the permission of the named insured.

Will Randy's policy cover Bob in this circumstance? Why or why not?

3. Assume instead that Randy's insurance policy defines "insureds" as:

> Any person while using the automobile provided that any such use of the automobile is with the permission of the named insured.

Will Randy's policy cover Bob in this circumstance? Why or why not?

Problem 132

Dave is nineteen years of age and lives at home. He drives his father's truck to work at the local supermarket everyday. His father has allowed him to use the truck on the express understanding that no one else should drive it and that Dave would follow a certain route to and from work. Dave's friend Billy is fourteen years of age. Billy is going to meet with Dave during his break, but arrives ten minutes early. It was cold outside the store, so Dave tossed Billy the car keys so that he could start the engine and keep warm. Billy listened to the radio for a few minutes but then got bored and drove off and was involved in an accident on the other side of town in which Spock suffered physical injuries. Deposition testimony indicated that on two previous occasions Dave had let Billy drive the truck.

Questions

1. Assume that Dave's father's insurance policy defines "insureds" as:

> Any person while operating the automobile provided the actual operation of the automobile is with the permission of the named insured.

Will the policy cover Billy in this circumstance? Why or why not?

2. Assume instead that Dave's father's insurance policy defines "insureds" as:

> Any person while using the automobile provided the actual use of the automobile is with the permission of the named insured.

Will the policy cover Billy in this circumstance? Why or why not?

3. Assume instead that Dave's father's insurance policy defines "insureds" as:

> Any person while using the automobile provided that any such use of the automobile is with the permission of the named insured.

Will the policy cover Billy in this circumstance? Why or why not?

4. In each of the above cases, what will Billy have to prove in order to obtain coverage?

5. Assume that, instead of an action for negligent driving being filed against Billy, the injured parties file an action against Dave claiming that his entrustment of the vehicle to Billy was negligent. How does your analysis under the three policies above change?

Problem 133

After touching down at the airport, Mavis Lawrence went inside the terminal to the International Rental Car Co. and rented a late model sedan. Conspicuously placed in the rental agreement signed by Mavis was the following language:

> The Vehicle shall NOT be operated by any person except the Customer who has signed this agreement. Customer expressly agrees not to permit use of the Vehicle by any other person without the prior written permission of International Rental Car Co.

All International Rental Car Co. vehicles are insured pursuant to local State Motor Vehicle Responsibility Laws which require insurance "for any person using any such motor vehicle with the express or implied permission of the named insured." After Mavis left the airport with the car, she met Sharon Lynch, a business associate, and the two of them headed toward a business meeting. Because she was tired from her airplane trip, Mavis let Sharon drive the rental car to the meeting while Mavis napped. On this drive, Lynch's negligence caused an accident and injury to Egger. Egger has now sued Lynch, who has turned the matter over to International's Insurance Co. for coverage. The company claims that Lynch is not an insured because of the violation by Mavis of the Rental Agreement. What result?

Problem 134

Dave Edwards, age 19, lived at home with his parents. Dave's parents owned a seven-year-old pickup truck and gave Dave permission to use the truck as Dave chose. Most of Dave's friends thought of the truck as "Dave's truck." Dave's father, however, had given Dave express instructions not to allow anyone to drive the truck. Dave had zealously followed that advice. One night, while

Dave had the truck out with some friends, Eric, a long-time friend of Dave, noticed the keys in the truck. Eric also saw his girlfriend in another car being driven by Albert. Eric told Dave that he, Eric, had to find out what was going on. Dave told Eric to go ahead, but that Dave could not go right then. Thinking that Dave had given him permission to use the truck, Eric jumped into the pickup and drove off. Seeing this, Dave yelled at Eric to stop. Eric yelled "don't worry" as he proceeded to smash the truck into the window of a downtown jewelry store. The jewelry store owner has filed suit against Eric. The pickup truck is insured by Dave's father's automobile policy which defines insureds as "anyone using the vehicle with the permission of the named insured." Eric, who lives at home with his parents, has no insurance, but Eric's father has two cars insured under a policy which provides coverage to members of Eric's father's household while using a non-owned vehicle "provided such use is with or reasonably believed to be with the permission of the owner of such non-owned vehicle."

Questions

1. Will Dave's father's insurance cover Eric?

2. Will Eric's father's insurance cover Eric?

3. Suppose both are obligated to cover the accident. How will coverage be divided?

Problem 135

Linda Altman lives at home with her mother. Mrs. Altman owns a five-year-old sedan which she insures. When Linda reached driving age, her mother gave Linda free use of the car whenever Mrs. Altman did not need it. Mrs. Altman, concerned with overly increasing her liability insurance costs, told Linda not to let others drive the car, but Mrs. Altman knew that on at least two occasions, Linda had allowed her friends to drive for short periods of time. One night, Linda told her mother that she was going out with Ginny, Linda's girlfriend, and that they were going to a party. In fact, Linda could not find the party and drove her mother's car instead to a local hamburger place. There she met Albert Mills. Mills claimed that he knew where the party was and ordered Linda to "scoot over." Mills jumped behind the wheel, pushed Linda over to the middle of the front seat and sped away, immediately crashing the car and injuring Ginny. Mrs. Altman's automobile insurance covers "any other person while operating the covered automobile provided their actual operation is with the express or implied permission of the named insured." Will the company be required to cover Mills?

Problem 136

Edward Anton drives his father's second car to work. His father has told Ed, "Do not let anyone else drive the car. I don't want your friends joyriding around in my car." At work, Ed became extremely busy on a complex project. Both Ed and his friend Delbert became hungry at lunchtime. Ed is slightly hypoglycemic and needs to eat at regular intervals. Because Ed was so busy, Delbert took Ed's keys and went out to get the two lunch. Delbert caused an accident while returning with lunch. Ed's father's automobile insurance policy covers "any other person while using the covered auto provided such use is with the permission of the named insured." Will Delbert's accident be covered?

PROBLEM 137

Employed by an automobile dealership, Andrea York has use of a "demonstrator" from the dealership. Her contract with the dealership provides:

> Employee shall use a "demonstrator" automobile assigned by Employer and shall use such vehicle, with price sticker and dealership named displayed, whenever possible in both employee and personal life.
>
> Employee SHALL NOT allow any non-employee of Employer to drive said automobile, unless such driver is a customer of Employer and such use is specifically authorized by employee's immediate supervisor.

When Andrea's own car was in the shop for repairs, Andrea allowed her daughter to drive the demonstrator to attend a night school class. Andrea figured it would be good publicity for the dealership to have this new car seen by college students. Daughter caused an accident near her college. The insurance policy of Andrea's employer provides coverage to the owner of the dealership as "named insured" and "to any other person using any covered auto provided their actual use is within the permission, express or implied, of the named insured." Will this insurance cover Daughter's accident?

Notes

R. HENDERSON, Insurance Law, *Motor Vehicle Accident Indemnification Corp. v. Continental National American Group Co.*, p. 454 (Michie, 1989); R. JERRY, Understanding Insurance Law, §51[b] (Matthew Bender, 1987); R. KEETON & A. WIDISS, Insurance Law, §4.7(b)(2) (West, 1988); R. KEETON, Basic Insurance Law, *Odolecki v. Hartford Acc. & Indem. Co.*, p. 338; *Motor Vehicle Acc.*

Indemnification Corp. v. Continental Nat'l Am. Group Co., p. 343; *Lukaszewicz v. Concrete Research, Inc.*, p. 346 (West, 1977); A. WIDISS, Insurance, *Riverside Ins. Co. of America v. Smith*, p. 322; note, pp. 330-31 (West, 1989); K. YORK & J. WHELAN, Insurance Law (Second Edition), *Metz v. Universal Underwriters Ins. Co.*, p. 21; note (and Statutes), pp. 594-96; *Curtis v. State Farm Mutual Automobile Ins. Co.*, p. 596; *Milbank Mutual Ins. Co. v. United States Fidelity and Guaranty Co.*, p. 601; note (and Statutes), pp. 606-608 (West, 1988); W. YOUNG & E. HOLMES, Insurance, *Subscribers v. McClanahan*, p. 350; notes, p. 355; *Motor Vehicle Accident Indemnification Corp. v. Continental National Group Co.*, p. 356; notes, pp. 358-59 (Foundation, 1985).

D. Uninsured Motorist Coverage

1. *Definitional Problems and Procedural Issues*

Problem 138

On a cold winter day in Franklin County, Ernie left home to go to the store only to find his pickup truck buried deep in a snowdrift. Undaunted, Ernie decided to walk. Halfway to his destination and while trying to walk in the street, Ernie was struck by a snowmobile being erratically driven by Cheryl. The snowmobile is owned by Kool Rental Co., which had rented it to Fred to go to the same store. While Fred was doing his shopping, Cheryl who is not related to Fred, had removed it. Ernie is severely injured. Ernie's insurance on his pickup truck has "Uninsured Motorist Protection" and provides that Ernie can recover up to $25,000 per person and $50,000 per accident [or more if the Insured's State requires more as a Statutory Minimum] for "damages which the insured is legally entitled to recover from the owner or operator of an uninsured motor vehicle because of bodily injury." Further investigation reveals that Fred has no insurance and that Kool Rental Co. has a liability insurance policy covering the snowmobiles which provides coverage in the amount of $10,000 for "any person driving a rental vehicle with the consent of the named insured."

Questions

1. When Ernie advised his insurance company of his injuries, the company advised that under no circumstances could a snowmobile be considered a "motor vehicle" within the meaning of the Uninsured Motorist coverage of the policy. Is this correct?

2. Assume that Ernie's Insurance Company is at least willing to listen, but that the snowmobile belonged to Ernie's estranged wife and Cheryl had stolen it from her home. What issues arise?

3. Assume that Cheryl was an employee of Kool Rental Co. and had been sent by her employer to remove the vehicle from Fred because of facts Kool learned after renting the snowmobile to Fred. Do any of your answers change?

Problem 139

Robert Steward took some time off from his college studies, left his dormitory room and went out riding his bicycle. He specifically recalls riding in what is clearly marked as a bicycle lane on the public street. He can also recall seeing a car over his left shoulder, can recall feeling a sharp pain, and can recall being thrown against a tree. He thinks he can recall hearing a car engine speed up like it was moving rapidly away. Robert does not own a car, but his mother does. Mother's insurance provides coverage for Uninsured Motorist and will pay a "covered person" any damages (up to the statutory minimum) which the person is entitled to recover as a result of being injured by an uninsured motor vehicle. The term "covered person" under the Uninsured Motorist Clause of the policy refers to the "named insured or any family member of the named insured."

Questions

1. Robert's mother's Insurance Co. refuses payment claiming that Robert is not a "covered person." What issue arises?

2. Robert's mother's Insurance Co. refuses payment claiming that because the car that forced Robert into the tree cannot be identified (Robert did file a hit and run report with the police), it cannot be determined if the driver was "uninsured." What result?

Problem 140

When her tire went suddenly flat on the Turnpike, Meghan Smith did the best she could to get the car all the way off the road. Unfortunately, a small portion of the rear of the car remained on the traveled portion. While Meghan was changing the flat driver's side front tire, she was struck and severely injured by a car driven by Bert Webster. Meghan's roommate owned the car Meghan was driving and had allowed Meghan to drive the car to work. Meghan's roommate had Uninsured Motorist Protection which defined "insured" to include: "Any other person while operating the covered motor vehicle."

Questions

1. Assume that Bert Webster has no automobile liability insurance. When she makes a claim to her roommate's insurance company for Uninsured Motorist coverage, Meghan is advised that she does not fit within the definition of "insured." Why? What result?

2. Assume that Bert Webster was covered by automobile insurance written by Flexible Insurance Co. The policy, written by one of Flexible's agents called for liability coverage to Bert in the amount of $10,000 per person and $20,000 per accident. State statute requires that any automobile insurance policy issued in the state be written in the statutory minimum amount of $25,000 and $50,000 per person. Meghan has general and special injuries which a jury would likely assess at $100,000. Thus, when Meghan learns about Webster's coverage, she makes a claim for Uninsured Motorist coverage to her roommate's insurance company. That Company argues that Bert has insurance and that this is really an underinsured motorist case, for which there is no coverage. What result?

3. Assume that Bert Webster was covered by automobile insurance written by Flexible Insurance Co. The policy, written by one of Flexible's agents called for liability coverage to Bert in the amount of $25,000 per person and $50,000 per accident. State statute requires that any automobile insurance policy issued in the state be written in the Statutory minimum amount of $25,000 and $50,000 per person. Meghan has general and special injuries which a jury would likely assess at $100,000. Thus, when Meghan learns about Webster's coverage, she makes a claim for Uninsured Motorist coverage to her roommate's insurance company. That Company argues that Bert has insurance

and that this is really an underinsured motorist case, for which there is no coverage. What result?

4. Assume that State Statute prescribes the obligations of all drivers following an accident and requires filing of a Proof of Financial Responsibility report with the Commissioner of Motor Vehicles indicating the name, address and other information about insurance coverage. Bert Webster apparently has coverage, but simply refuses to file the required report. After her claim for UM coverage is turned down by Meghan's roommate's insurance company because there is no proof that Webster is uninsured, Meghan argues that failure to file proof of Financial Responsibility is presumptive evidence of Webster's status as an uninsured motorist. Will this argument be successful?

5. Assume that Bert Webster resides in another state. The name and address that he leaves with police following the accident turn out to be false and, as a result, Meghan's lawyer is simply unable to serve civil process on Webster. Because Meghan has been unable to obtain personal service over Webster, she makes a claim against her roommate's Uninsured Motorist provision. The insurance company defends this claim on the basis that Webster is not uninsured. What result?

6. Assume that Bert Webster was actually trying to run Meghan down as a result of a business argument the two had. Webster's policy with Flexible Insurance provides coverage well in excess of the statutory minimum but when sued by Meghan Flexible takes the position that Webster's actions were intentional and, therefore, not covered. Can Meghan now make a claim under her roommate's Uninsured Motorist coverage?

PROBLEM 141

While riding to the train station with his wife, Carl Frederich was seriously injured when his wife negligently drove the car off the road. Carl has an automobile policy which covers the car which Carl's wife was driving. That policy defines as "insured" "the named insured and any residents of the household of the named insured." The policy also provides, under "EXCLUSIONS: "This policy does not apply under the liability provisions to the liability of any insured for bodily injury to the named insured." The policy also provides Uninsured Motorist Protection. How can Carl obtain coverage for his injuries?

PROBLEM 142

Duke was driving downtown with Kitty, his common law wife, and John, his son by a previous marriage. John was serving in the coast-guard and had been stationed in Los Angeles for two years. Duke let John out of the car near the stadium so that he could meet up with his friends. As Duke was pulling away from the curb, he realized that the tire had a puncture. He stopped, called John back to help and asked Kitty to use a nearby phone to contact a gas station. Oliver, a policeman, stopped behind Duke's car, left his cruiser and directed traffic around the disabled vehicle, while John and Duke pulled the spare tire from the trunk. Just as Kitty arrived back with news of a tow-truck's impending arrival, George, an uninsured motorist, crashed into Duke's car injuring Duke, Kitty, John and Oliver.

Duke's policy with New Guard included un(der)insured motorist coverage which defined "insured" as: (i) the named insured and, while residents of the same household, the spouse and relative of the named insured; (ii) any other person while occupying the insured motor vehicle." The definition section of the policy qualified "occupying" as "in or upon or entering into or alighting from."

Questions

1. The injured parties all make claims against New Guard. How should those claims be resolved?

2. Assume that George was a hit-and-run driver who was never apprehended or identified. What new issue now arises for consideration?

Problem 143

Joshua Abbott was seriously injured in an automobile accident when Abbott's car was struck from behind by a car driven by David Lawrence. Lawrence, whose license was already revoked, admitted to police that he had no insurance. He was convicted under a state statute making it a misdemeanor to operate a vehicle without insurance. Lawrence has no income and owns no property other than the automobile he was driving, which automobile was wrecked in the crash with Abbott. Abbott has automobile insurance with Faithful Insurance Co., which insurance includes a provision for Uninsured Motorist protection. Abbott has now made claim to Faithful under the UM provisions for his injuries.

Questions

1. When Faithful refuses to even listen to Abbott, Abbott files suit against Faithful for the damages Abbott sustained in the accident with Lawrence. Faithful seeks to dismiss this action as failing to state a claim upon which relief can be granted because Abbott has not sued Lawrence for the injuries. What result on this motion?

2. Assume that Abbott sues Lawrence for his injuries and joins Faithful in the same action. Faithful moves for dismissal of this claim because Abbott has not first sought arbitration of the claim with Faithful. What result on this motion?

3. Assume that Abbott does have the right to file suit against Faithful. Abbott's policy provides that "any suit against the Company arising out of the Uninsured Motorist Coverage must be filed against us within 1 year of the date of the accident." State statute of limitations provide a limitations period of two years for tort actions and four years for contract actions. When must Abbott file suit against the Co?

4. Assume that Abbott is required to file suit against the Company under the contract statute of limitations in question 3. He thus files suit three years following the accident. Abbott did not sue Lawrence in this or any other action. Faithful now seeks to dismiss the claim, with prejudice. What result?

5. If Faithful pays any money to Abbott, does Faithful acquire any rights as to Lawrence?

Notes

E. FISCHER & P. SWISHER, Principles of Insurance Law, Uninsured Motorist Coverage, p. 440; Notes & questions, p. 443; *Calvert v. Farmers Ins. Co. of Arizona*, p. 726 (Matthew Bender, 1986); R.

HENDERSON, Insurance Law, *State Farm Mut. Ins. Co. v. Brudnock*, p. 270; notes, pp. 274-76 (Michie, 1989); R. JERRY, Understanding Insurance Law, §133 (Matthew Bender, 1987); R. KEETON & A. WIDISS, Insurance Law, §§4.9(e), 4.7(c) (West, 1988); R. KEETON, Basic Insurance Law, *Taylor v. Great Central Ins. Co.*, p. 115; A Study in Standardization, pp. 117-19; *MacBey v. Hartford Accident & Indemnity Co.*, p. 352; *Bachman v. Independence Indemnity Co.*, p. 354 (West, 1977); A. WIDISS, Insurance, Uninsured Motorist Insurance, pp. 101-105; 358-59; 369-371; *Pin Pin H Su v. Kemper Ins. Co.*, p. 423; McGlynn v. Safeco Ins. Co. of America , p. 669 (West, 1989); K. YORK & J. WHELAN, Insurance Law (Second Edition), *Pin Pin H. Su v. Kemper Insurance Companies/American Motorists Ins. Co.*, p. 23; *Votedian v. General Accident Fire & Life Assurance Corp.*, p. 713 (West, 1988); W. YOUNG & E. HOLMES, Insurance, *Mutual of Enumclaw Ins. Co. v. Wiscomb*, p. 91 (Foundation, 1985).

2. *Stacking*

PROBLEM 144

While driving down the street one icy winter day, Davis Mallen saw a car approaching his car from the opposite direction. All of a sudden, the other car crossed the center line and started heading directly at Mallen. Mallen sounded his horn, steered to his right, and attempted to apply the brakes. As he moved closer to the side of the road, the car hit a patch of ice, Mallen skidded off the road, over the sidewalk and into the front window of Pace's Hardware Store. The other car kept on going. Although these actions were seen by several eyewitnesses, none of those witnesses were able to read the license number of the car and, as a result, it went unidentified. In the resulting collision, Davis Mallen was severely injured and required hospitalization. Additionally, Pace's Hardware Store suffered extensive structural damage. Mallen owns three vehicles, including the one he was driving at the time of the accident. Each vehicle is insured by Reliable Insurance Co. and provides liability insurance in the amount of $25,000 for each person, $50,000 for each occurrence, $5,000 medical payments and Uninsured Motorist coverage in the amounts of $25,000/$50,000. Mallen pays a separate premium for each car for each of these coverages. After he was released from the hospital, Mallen received bills from the hospital and doctors for $9,500 as well as a bill from Pace's Hardware Store for $40,000 for the damage to the structure. Mallen still has major residual pain and suffering left from his injuries and your best guess is that a jury would assess his injuries in the $125,000 to $150,000 range.

Because Mallen is the named insured on the policy for each of his three cars, and because he obviously had permission to drive another one of his cars, can Mallen obtain separate coverage for his liability, medical, and UM claims from each of the three policies?

Problem 145

For fifteen years, No Fault Inc. has been writing Personal Injury Protection (P.I.P.) in Northstate. Northstate statute had expressly denied the stacking of P.I.P. coverages.

Under Insurance Co. is No Fault Inc.'s wholly-owned subsidiary through which it intends to write automobile coverage outside of the no fault states. In each of these states, the legislation is silent and the courts have not decided whether to permit stacking of Uninsured Motorist coverage. We have been asked to identify, in the form of a short memorandum, some of the issues that arise in the area of stacking. Specifically, we have been asked to deal with the following points:

1.) In the following examples the claimant has suffered personal injury damages in excess of the sum of total coverages available. In each of the following examples, the claimant is injured by an uninsured automobile and attempts to recover under each of the uninsured automobile coverages which are mentioned. Identify the type of stacking involved in each example.

a) Eric is a named (class I) insured on a policy with Big Insurance Co. He is a passenger in Fred's automobile and, hence an occupancy (class II) insured under Fred's policy with Little Insurance Co when he incurs his damages.

b) Eric is a named insured on a policy with Big Insurance Co. Eric insures both his automobiles under this policy. Eric's wife is the injured claimant.

c) Eric is a named insured on a policy on his car with Big Insurance Co. His wife's car is insured with Little Insurance Co. Eric is walking down the street when he is struck by an uninsured motorist.

d) Eric does not own an automobile. He is injured while a passenger in Fred's automobile. Fred has insured that vehicle with Big Insurance Co. Fred has insured his other automobile with Little Insurance Co.

2.) The following are three examples of clauses that other insurers have utilized in order to impede stacking of un(der)insured coverages.

> a) With respect to bodily injury to an insured while occupying a vehicle not owned by the named insured, this insurance shall apply only as excess insurance over any other similar insurance available to such insured and applicable to such vehicle as primary insurance, and this insurance shall then apply only in the amount by which the limit of liability for this coverage exceeds the applicable limit of such other insurance.

b) Except as provided in the foregoing paragraph, if the insured has other similar insurance available and applicable to the accident, the damages shall be deemed not to exceed the higher of the applicable limits of liability of this insurance and such other insurance, and the company shall not be liable for a greater proportion of any loss to which this coverage applies than the limit of liability hereunder bears to the sum of the applicable limits of liability of this insurance and such other insurance.

c) Regardless of the number of insureds under this policy, the company's liability is as follows:

The limit of liability stated in the schedule as applicable to 'each person' is the limit of the company's liability for all damages because of bodily injury sustained by one person as the result of any one accident ***.

Underinsurance Co. has asked us to describe these clauses. Against which particular species of stacking is each of these clauses particularly targeted? What type of legislation could defeat all or any of them.

3.) What are the major arguments in favor of holding anti-stacking clauses to be invalid. Do these arguments apply with equal force to all of the above types of clause. In particular, should the "limits of liability" clause be treated differently from the "other insurance" clauses?

Problem 146

Anne Marshall owns two motor vehicles: a 2 year old motorcycle and a 1 year old sportscar. Each of these vehicles is separately insured under an automobile policy written by Heritage Insurance Co. Each policy contains Uninsured Motorist Coverage for each vehicle in the amounts of $25,000 per person and $50,000 per occurrence. Anne pays separate premiums for each of these coverages. In addition, Anne owns a 2 year old station wagon jointly with her father. There is an insurance policy on that vehicle written by Angel Insurance Co., which Father holds, but which lists Anne and Father as named insureds. It has UM coverage in the same $25,000/$50,000 amounts. Anne does not live with her father.

Questions

1. Assume that Anne and Father are involved in an accident with an uninsured motorist while Anne is driving the motorcycle. Father has injuries which are reasonably calculated at $60,000. How much should Father collect and from whom?

2. Assume that Anne is also seriously injured in the same accident. Anne has injuries which are reasonably calculated at $75,000. How much should Anne collect and from whom?

3. Assume in Question 2. that the policy on the Station Wagon written by Angel Insurance Co. has a clause which provides:

> We do not provide uninsured motorist coverage to any covered person while occupying a motor vehicle which is owned by an insured which is not insured for uninsured motorist coverage under this policy.

Will this clause be enforced against Anne?

4. Assume that the policy on the motorcycle provided as follows:

> In the event that there is any other uninsured motorist coverage available from any other source, the uninsured

> motorist coverage provided in this policy shall be "excess" over any other such insurance.

Will this clause affect any of your answers to Question 1?

5. Assume, in Question 4, that Father had only $30,000 worth of injuries. How does this affect your answer?

Notes

E. FISCHER & P. SWISHER, Principles of Insurance Law, *Cardin v. Royal Ins. Co. of America*, p. 441; *Rusthoven v. Commercial Standard Ins. Co.*, p. 568 (Matthew Bender, 1986); R. JERRY, Understanding Insurance Law, §§135D[a], [c] (Matthew Bender, 1987); R. KEETON & A. WIDISS, Insurance Law, §§5.9, 3.11(f) (West, 1988); R. KEETON, Basic Insurance Law, *Werley v. United Services Automobile Ass'n.*, p. 255; *Hardware Dealers Mut. Fire Ins. Co. v. Farmers Ins. Exchange*, p. 263 (West, 1977); A. WIDISS, Insurance, *Mission Ins. Co. v. United States Fire Ins. Co.*, p. 243; *Dullenty v. Rocky Mountain Fire & Cas. Co.*, p. 360; 674; Limits of Liability Provisions, p. 541; *Bilodeau v. Lumbermen's Mut. Cas. Co.*, p. 542; "Stacking" Multiple Units, p. 546; *Rusthoven v. Commercial Standard Ins. Co.*, p. 547; 638 (West, 1989); K. YORK & J. WHELAN, Insurance Law (Second Edition), *Wagner v. State Farm Mutual Automobile Ins. Co.*, p. 700; *Estate of Rosato v. Harleysville Mutual Ins. Co.*, p. 707; *Providence Washington Insurance Co. v. Rosato*, p. 711 (West, 1988).

E. Special Problems of No Fault Insurance

Problem 147

Ms. Mitchell is the owner of an automobile insured by Canyon Insurance. The policy provided personal injury protection. She permitted her estranged husband, David, to operate the vehicle while she and her sons Graham and Steven were passengers. David intentionally drove off the highway and the vehicle plunged down a cliff. Graham and Steven survived but were seriously injured. They claimed their medical expenses and lost incomes under the Canyon policy.

The Anystate personal injury protection legislation provides:

(a) No automobile liability insurance policy . . . covering liability arising out of the ownership, maintenance, or use of any automobile or motorcycle shall be delivered in this state unless personal injury protection is included therein . . .

(b) Personal Injury Protection consists of provisions of coverage which provide for payment to the named insured and members of the insured's household, any authorized operator or passenger of the named insured's motor vehicle including a guest occupant, up to an amount of $5,000 for each such person for payment of all reasonable expenses arising from the accident . . .

(c) The benefits required herein shall be payable without regard to the fault or non-fault of the named insured or the recipient in causing or contributing to the accident . . .

(k) Insurers may exclude a person from benefits under this act where such person's conduct contributed to his personal injuries or death occurred . . . (iii) while acting with specific intent of causing injury or damage to himself or others.

Questions

1. Advise Graham and Steven as to what arguments may be made in their favor and how the court will deal with the issues presented.

2. How crucial is explicit policy language when a court deals with a question of interpretation regarding modern mandatory insurance coverage?

3. Legislative interest in mandatory insurance has shifted focus from third party (liability coverage) to first party plans (un(der)insured and no-fault systems). How would you expect that to impact upon the courts' approaches to intentionally caused injuries? Would you expect specific legislation on this issue?

Problem 148

Driving by the lake after a substantial storm, Andrew Sands did not see that the road ahead was flooded. He drove his car into the flooded area and, before he could do anything, the car was swept over a guard rail and into the lake. Sands, apparently stunned, was able to free himself from the car, but drowned as he attempted to reach shore. Under the Personal Injury Protection Benefits of Sands' automobile insurance policy, Sands widow would be entitled to receive payment for the economic losses resulting from "accidental bodily injury sustained while the insured was occupying the motor vehicle."

Questions

1. Will Mrs. Sands receive benefits under her late husband's policy?

2. Assume that Sands was uninsured and that his car was swept through the wall of a home injuring the homeowner, who was asleep at the time. Would the homeowner be considered a "pedestrian" for the purpose of the homeowner's own automobile PIP coverage?

Notes

E. FISCHER & P. SWISHER, Principles of Insurance Law, No-Fault Automobile Insurance, p. 562; *Antanovich v. Allstate Ins. Co.*, p. 563; notes & questions, pp. 567-68; No-Fault Insurance, p. 730; *Barcena v. Hawaiian & Guaranty Co., Ltd.*, p. 730; notes & questions, pp. 735-36 (Matthew Bender, 1986); R. HENDERSON, Insurance Law, *Thornton v. Allstate Ins. Co.*, p. 254; notes, p. 260 (Michie, 1989); R. KEETON & A. WIDISS, Insurance Law, §4.10 (West, 1988); R. KEETON, Basic Insurance Law, *Montgomery v. Daniels*, p. 365; policy forms, pp. 378-382 (West, 1977); A. WIDISS, Insurance, *Allstate Ins. Co. v. Reitler*, p. 227; No-Fault Motor Vehicle Insurance, pp. 371-79; *Farmers Ins. Exchange v. Call*, p. 683 (West, 1989); K. YORK & J. WHELAN, Insurance Law (Second Edition), Note, New York's No Fault Scheme, pp. 18-20 (West, 1988); W. YOUNG & E. HOLMES, Insurance, *State Farm Fire & Cas. Co. v. Tringali*, p. 125; notes, pp. 129-130; *Bituminous Cas. Corp. v. Mowery*, p. 405; note 2, p. 409 (Foundation, 1985).

Chapter Nine

The Claims Process

A. The Duty of Cooperation by the Insured

Note

Problems 149-154 are based on the following Statement of Facts.

Statement of Facts

Late on a warm evening in the middle of last August, Kelly McGovern, the manager of the Montvale Monarchs, America's newest major league baseball franchise, was having a few drinks in an L.A. tavern following the Monarch's 12-0 loss to the Dodgers. The loss, the Monarchs nineteenth in a row, was particularly painful because Lefty Wright, McGovern's All Star pitcher had thrown seven scoreless innings until his arm tightened up in the top of the eighth. McGovern's pitiful bullpen and questionable defense then allowed 12 runs on 5 hits, 4 errors, 4 walks and a hit batter in the bottom of the eighth inning. Thus, when Sam Finley, a slightly drunk patron in the tavern, recognized McGovern and began riding him about the Monarchs, McGovern became upset and asked Finley to please keep quiet. Matters got out of hand when Finley responded that "Not even Sandy Koufax could help your club." McGovern and Finley were soon engaged in heated conversation. Before too much time had elapsed, Finley wound up on the floor, severely injured. Finley has now sued McGovern claiming that his injuries are McGovern's fault. McGovern has turned the suit papers over to Golden Coverage Insurance Company, which writes liability insurance for McGovern as part of his Homeowner's Insurance. The policy has a clause which provides:

> ***Assistance and Cooperation of the Insured.*** The Insured shall cooperate with the Company and upon the Company's request shall assist in making settlements, in the conduct of suits and in enforcing any right of contribution or indemnity against any person who may be liable to the Insured because of bodily injury and property damage. The Insured shall attend hearings and trials and shall assist in securing and giving evidence and obtaining the attendance of witnesses.

Problem 149

Following receipt of the suit papers from McGovern, Golden Coverage's adjuster, Francis Marley called McGovern and told him that Golden Coverage needed to question McGovern under oath regarding his side of the case. McGovern told Marley, "I don't have a 'side;' I just tell the truth. If you want answers, you ought to call Finley and ask him." Is McGovern required to submit to such questioning? What if he refuses? Must McGovern prove that he cooperated or must Golden Coverage prove that he did not?

Problem 150

After Golden Coverage processed the suit papers received from McGovern, Francis Marley, the adjuster handling the case, wrote McGovern:

> Dear Mr. McGovern:
>
> We need to question you about the incident with Mr. Finley. I have assigned the investigation to Mr. Mike Owens, our chief investigator and he will question you at 4:00 p.m. on October 3.
>
> Sincerely yours,
>
> Francis Marley
>
> Golden Coverage Ins.

In fact, Mike Owens waited at Golden Coverage Insurance Company's headquarters until 5:00 p.m. on October 3, but McGovern never appeared. Assuming that there is prejudice to the insurance company when it cannot interview its own insured, is McGovern's failure to appear a breach of the cooperation clause? Why or why not?

Problem 151

After Golden Coverage became involved in the *Finley v. McGovern* matter, it had its chief investigator, Mike Owens interview McGovern. Owens, who was unfamiliar with the file in the matter, asked McGovern: "Now, when does your policy expire?" Outraged at such questions, McGovern said: "I don't have to answer such stupid questions." McGovern refused to answer this question. Is this failure a breach of the cooperation clause? Why or why not?

PROBLEM 152

After investigating the incident, Golden Coverage decided to defend McGovern in the action by Finley, and assigned one of its staff attorneys to handle the matter. The attorney advised McGovern of the trial date two months before the actual date. When he received that information, McGovern wrote back to the attorney and advised that the Monarchs would be playing in New York on that date and that he simply could not possibly attend court. Even though the attorney advised Golden Coverage of this problem, Golden Coverage did nothing, and McGovern did not appear for trial. Is this a breach of the cooperation clause? Why or why not?

PROBLEM 153

After investigating the incident, Golden Coverage decided to defend McGovern in the action by Finley, and assigned one of its staff attorneys to handle the matter. The attorney advised McGovern of the trial date two months before the actual date. McGovern wrote down the date in his date book, but accidentally wrote down the wrong date. On the actual date of trial, McGovern was with the Monarchs in New York and, as a result, the attorney could not reach him. The case was tried in McGovern's absence and McGovern lost. Is this a breach of the cooperation clause? Why or why not?

Problem 154

After investigating the incident, Golden Coverage decided to defend McGovern in the action by Finley, and assigned one of its staff attorneys to handle the matter. The attorney advised McGovern of the trial date two months before the actual date. While acknowledging the date, McGovern refused to participate, still believing that the entire incident was Finley's fault. He refused to attend the trial. Is this conduct a breach of the cooperation clause? Why or why not?

Notes

E. FISCHER & P. SWISHER, Principles of Insurance Law, *Home Indemnity Co. v. Reed Equipment Co.*, p. 493; notes & questions, pp. 497-98; *Fine v. Bellefonte Underwriters Ins. Co.*, p. 498; notes & questions, pp. 501-502; *Travelers Insurance Co. v. Godsey*, p. 502; notes & questions, p. 505; *Newport v. MFA Insurance Co.*, p. 515 (Matthew Bender, 1986); R. HENDERSON, Insurance Law, *Hoekstra v. Farm Bureau Mutual Ins. Co.*, p. 654; notes, pp. 660-61; *Continental Ins. Co. v. Bayless & Roberts, Inc. p. 678* (Michie, 1989); R. JERRY, Understanding Insurance Law, §§85; 110 (Matthew Bender, 1987); R. KEETON & A. WIDISS, Insurance Law, §7.3 (West, 1988); R. KEETON, Basic Insurance Law, *Western Mutual Ins. Co. v. Baldwin*, p. 776; *Members Mutual Ins. Co. v. Cutaia*, p. 787; *Oregon Automobile Ins. Co. v. Salzberg*, p. 812; *Coleman v. New Amsterdam Casualty Co.*, p. 816; *Farm & City Ins. Co. v. Hassel*, p. 816; *American Fire & Casualty Co. v. Vliet*, p. 821 (West, 1977); A. WIDISS, Insurance, Assistance and Cooperations Provisions, p. 735 (West, 1989); K. YORK & J. WHELAN, Insurance Law (Second Edition), Introductory note, pp. 521-22; note 2, p. 528; *Dietz v. Hardware Dealers Mutual Fire Ins. Co., p. 631* (West, 1988); W. YOUNG & E. HOLMES, Insurance, *MFA Mutual Ins. Co. v. Sailors*, p. 332; notes, pp. 334-36; The Sequel to *Sailors*, p. 336; notes, pp. 337-38; *Tibbs v. Johnson*, p. 338 (Foundation, 1985).

B. Duty to Pay/Duty to Defend

Problem 155

As a result of a disagreement over which Presidential candidate would better suit the needs of the American people, Billy Turnbow and Robert Humphrey got into a pushing match. When Turnbow decided to break off the altercation and turned to leave, he was struck from behind by a blunt instrument and sent crashing to the ground. He sustained a concussion and various other injuries and has sought to recover for those injuries from Humphrey. Humphrey is covered by a personal liability insurance policy with the All Hands Insurance Co. That policy covers Humphrey for "all sums which the insured shall become legally obligated to pay as a damages because of an occurrence." The policy then defines "occurrence" as "an accident which is neither expected nor intended from the standpoint of the insured." Finally, the policy provides that in the event of an "occurrence" covered by the policy, All Hands "will 1.) pay up to our limit of liability for the damages for which the insured is legally liable and 2.) provide a defense at our expense by counsel of our choice." This same clause then allows All Hands the option to try the suit or to negotiate a settlement of any claim.

Humphrey has sent Turnbow's petition for damages on to All Hands and has requested that the company both defend him in the action and pay any judgment.

Questions

1. Assume that Turnbow's complaint alleged that Humphrey "intentionally struck Turnbow" and that injuries resulted. Can All Hands Insurance Co. refuse to provide a defense to the action and indicate to Humphrey that it will not pay any judgment obtained by Turnbow?

2. Assume that, in addition, local pleading rules allow a complaint to be amended at any time up to and including the time of trial. Does this change your answer in any way?

3. Assume that the complaint of Turnbow alleged that Humphrey's action was "reckless, willful, wanton and with careless disregard for the safety of Turnbow." Does this change your answer?

4. Assume that the pleading stated that Humphrey "intentionally" struck Turnbow, but the adjuster handling the case for All Hands received news accounts of the matter from a local paper indicating that Humphrey had actually interceded in an argument between Turnbow and two other persons and that, in the confusion, Turnbow had slipped and fallen. Does All Hands have any obligation to defend or pay?

5. Assume that the pleading simply indicated that Humphrey "caused Turnbow to be thrown to the floor causing Turnbow severe injuries." Does All Hands have any obligation to defend or pay?

6. Assume in the preceding question that the adjuster for All Hands also had sworn affidavits from several witnesses indicating that Humphrey had, unprovoked, grabbed Turnbow and threw him to the ground. Does this change

your answer?

7. Assume that when All Hands received the complaint, it alleged that Humphrey acted intentionally, but Humphrey has told All Hands that these allegations were not true. All Hands refuses to make any inquiries of any witnesses and denies defense or coverage. Is this correct?

8. Assume that the complaint alleged that Humphrey acted intentionally in count I, but alleged that he acted negligently in count II. What are All Hands obligations?

9. Assume that the complaint alleged that Humphrey acted intentionally and All Hands refused to defend. Just prior to trial, Turnbow's lawyer is granted permission to amend the complaint to allege negligence. Does All Hands have any obligations?

10. Assume that All Hands agrees to defend the case. Humphrey's policy has a limit of $25,000 for damages. Turnbow has alleged $50,000 worth of injuries. If All Hands pays Turnbow the $25,000, can it refuse to further defend the case?

11. Assume that All Hands provides a defense and that Humphrey loses. Humphrey wants to appeal the result. Is All Hands obligated to pursue an appeal?

12. Assume that Humphrey has another liability policy in addition to the one already discussed in these questions. This second policy, with First State Insurance Company, would also cover Humphrey for an occurrence of this type. When All Hands refused to defend, Humphrey sent the case to First State, which did agree to defend the case. Assuming that both the All Hands and the First State policies are pro rata policies, does First State have any claim

against All Hands for contribution to the defense of the matter?

Problem 156

Mary Big had a personal liability policy with Forthright Insurance Company which provided Mary with $25,000 worth of liability protection. After causing several injuries, Mary submitted suit papers on those claims to Forthright, which responded by saying that Mary was not covered for the loss incurred. As a result, Forthright denied Mary's claim for coverage. Mary Big has come in to your office with the suit papers and you are convinced that the insurance company is wrong in denying a defense to the claims. Your calls to the insurance company have not, however, changed Forthright's decision. As a result, Mary has asked the following questions:

Questions

1. How can Mary test whether Forthright is obligated to defend her?

2. Assuming that the cases against Mary go to trial, must Mary hire a lawyer to defend her? What if she does not and allows a default to be entered against her?

3. Assume that a judgment goes against Mary and that she subsequently sues Forthright for wrongfully denying her a defense. Can Forthright defend by saying that, following Forthright's denial, Mary failed to send copies of new suit papers to Forthright thereby breaching her obligation of cooperation?

4. Assume that a judgment is entered against Mary in the underlying

lawsuit in the amount of $100,000. It is later determined that Forthright wrongfully denied Mary a defense in the action. What are Mary's damages?

Notes

E. FISCHER & P. SWISHER, Principles of Insurance Law, *McFadyen v. North River Ins. Co.*, p. 506; notes & questions, pp. 509-510; *Omark Industries, Inc. v. Safeco Ins. Co. of America*, p. 510 (Matthew Bender, 1986); R. HENDERSON, Insurance Law, *Lanoue v. Fireman's Fund American Ins. Co.*, p. 664; *Ruder & Finn, Inc. v. Seaboard Surety Co.*, p. 671; notes, pp. 671-73; *Ramos v. Northwestern Mut. Ins. Co.*, p. 673; notes, pp. 677-78; *Continental Ins. Co. v. Bayless & Roberts, Inc.*, p. 678; notes, pp. 690-91; *Thornton v. Paul*, p. 691; notes, pp. 703-704; *Mannheimer Bros. v. Kansas Casualty & Surety Co.*, p. 704; notes, p. 706-707; *Kocse v. Liberty Mut. Ins. Co.*, p. 707; notes, pp. 710-11; *Smith v. American Family Mut. Ins. Co.*, p. 756; notes, p. 765 (Michie, 1989); R. JERRY, Understanding Insurance Law, §§111; 113 (Matthew Bender, 1987); R. KEETON & A. WIDISS, Insurance Law, §§7.6(a),(b),(d) (West, 1988); R. KEETON, Basic Insurance Law, *Conner v. Transamerica Ins. Co.*, p. 822; *Hawkeye-Security Ins. Co. v. Indemnity Ins. Co.*, p. 829; *Glens Falls Group Ins. Corp. v. Hoium*, p. 832; *Burd v. Sussex Mutual Ins. Co.*, p. 837 (West, 1977); A. WIDISS, Insurance, The Liability of First Party Insurers for Consequential Damages, p. 773; *Hoskins v. Aetna Life Ins. Co.*, p. 774; 786; *Murphy v. Cincinnati Ins. Co.*, p. 778; The Liability Insurer's Duty and Right to Defend, p. 802; *Gray v. Zurich Ins. Co.*, p. 805; *Auto-Owners Ins. Co. v. Transamerica Ins. Co.*, p. 817; Determining the Obligation to Provide Defense, p. 819; *Maryland Casualty Co. v. Peppers*, p. 821; *Brown v. State Automobile & Cas. Underwriters*, p. 825; Discharging the Insurer's Obligation to Provide a Defense, p. 840; *Anderson v. U.S. Fidelity & Guarantee Co.*, p. 840; *Commercial Union Ins. Co. v. Pittsburgh Corning Corp.*, p. 842; *Gross v. Lloyds of London Ins. Co.*, p. 848; Remedies, p. 855; *Green v. J.C. Penney Auto Ins. Co., Inc.*, p. 856 (West, 1989); K. YORK & J. WHELAN, Insurance Law (Second Edition), Preliminary Note, pp. 628-631; *Stockdale v. Jamison*, p. 642; note, pp. 649-650; *Smith v. American Family Mutual Ins. Co.*, p. 650; *Mullen v. Glens Falls Ins. Co.*, p. 658 (West, 1988); W. YOUNG & E. HOLMES, Insurance, *Afcan v. Mutual Fire, Marine & Inland Ins. Co.*, p. 277; notes, pp. 284-85; *Gray v. Zurich Ins. Co.*, p. 286; notes, pp. 292-94 (Foundation, 1985).

C. Reservation of Rights/Non-Waiver Agreements

Problem 157

Following a football game at which he was a spectator, David Trane was involved in a scuffle with several fans of the opposing team. In the scuffle, Trane somehow struck and injured Matt Dean, one of the opposing fans. Dean has now sued Trane for damages in the amount of $75,000 as a result of the fight. Trane has sent the complaint to Bigg Insurance Company, which insures Trane's home and provides him with personal liability insurance in the amount of $50,000. Upon reading the complaint, the adjuster for Bigg is unsure whether the complaint alleges that Trane's striking of Dean was intentional or negligent. Because of the circumstances, however, the adjuster believes that the incident resulted from an intentional act and would thus be excluded from coverage under the policy. You are attorney for Bigg Insurance and have been asked to respond to the following questions:

Questions

1. Can Bigg undertake defense of the complaint for Trane with the idea of developing information from which Bigg can later assert that there was no coverage for the incident?

2. If Bigg undertakes defense of the complaint, can it later assert that the incident was not covered?

3. If Bigg decides to write a Reservation of Rights letter to Trane, what should the letter include?

4. Assume that, at the time Bigg decides to write a Reservation of Rights letter, Bigg does not know enough facts to determine the likelihood of coverage. How can it proceed by letter and still protect itself?

5. How does a Reservation of Rights letter differ from a Non-Waiver Agreement?

6. Is a court more likely to enforce a Reservation of Rights letter or a Non-Waiver Agreement? Why?

7. Assume that either a Reservation of Rights Letter or Non-Waiver

Agreement is executed. Thereafter, Bigg's adjuster learns of new, additional reasons for denying coverage. Under what circumstances can these new circumstances be used to deny coverage?

8. Assume that Bigg proceeds to defend Trane under a reservation of rights. Who has the right to settle the action under the express terms of the cooperation clause?

9. Assume that, following the trial, Bigg decides that the actions of Trane were indeed intentional and that Bigg is not obligated to pay the judgment obtained. Does it have any obligation to Trane in this regard?

10. OPTIONAL PROBLEM--At the direction of the Instructor, draft the Reservation of Rights letters which you would advise the Bigg adjuster to send to Trane in connection with Questions 3 above, together with the Non-Waiver Agreement referred to in Question 4 above.

Notes

Note for Optional Problem 10. Only. *See* J. Appleman, Insurance Law & Practice, §§12036-12037 (1980).

Problem 158

Tony and Ward went out on a drinking binge. They both consumed prodigious quantities of alcohol. Ward was driving them home in his automobile when he misjudged a curve and crashed, severely injuring Tony. Ward had automobile liability coverage in the amount of $25,000 per person and $50,000 per accident with Practical Insurance Inc. Ward had also purchased a personal policy of excess liability coverage with defendant Excessover Insurance Company in the amount of $500,000. The Excessover but not the Practical policy contained an express clause excluding coverage in the event that the insured driver was intoxicated.

Practical Insurance defended Ward in a negligence action brought by Tony. Tony's counsel did not base his allegation of negligence on Ward's allegedly intoxicated state. Ward's counsel originally had asserted a fault defense against Tony based on Tony's knowledge of Ward's alleged intoxication but subsequently had withdrawn that defense. Ward was found liable in the underlying negligence action in the amount of $150,000 and Tony has requested payment of the excess damages from Excessover.

Excessover wishes to litigate the issue of non-coverage, and allege that its intoxication exclusion applies to Ward. Tony argues that Excessover is estopped from litigating the issue of coverage.

Specifically, Tony argues, first, that Excessover is estopped because it failed to obtain a reservation of rights or execute a nonwaiver agreement. Second, Tony argues that Excessover was estopped because the issues had been litigated in the underlying tort action.

How should the court rule on Tony's claims?

Notes

E. FISCHER & P. SWISHER, Principles of Insurance Law, *Draft Systems, Inc. v. Alspach*, p. 309; notes & questions, pp. 311-12 (Matthew Bender, 1986);R. JERRY, Understanding Insurance Law, §114[c][2] (Matthew Bender, 1987); R. KEETON & A. WIDISS, Insurance Law, §6.7(a) (West, 1988); R. KEETON, Basic Insurance Law, *Burd v. Sussex Mutual Ins. Co.*, p. 837; questions (1) & (2), p. 847 (West, 1977); A. WIDISS, Insurance, Avoiding or Limiting Claims for Variance; Reservation-of-Rights Notices and Non-Waiver Agreements, p. 712; *United States Automobile Assoc. v. Morris*, p. 856 (West, 1989); K. YORK & J. WHELAN, Insurance Law (Second Edition), *Smith v. American Family Mutual Ins. Co.*, p. 650; *United*

Services Automobile Ass'n. v. Morris, p. 667 (West, 1988); W. YOUNG & E. HOLMES, Insurance, *Raymond v. Georgia Farm Mut. Ins. Co.*, p. 309; Reservations and Nonwaivers, p. 312; notes, pp. 314-15 (Foundation, 1985).

D. SETTLEMENT PRACTICES

1. Duty of Insurer

PROBLEM 159

Several weeks ago, Dave Davis agreed to take his daughter and the daughter of his next door neighbor to the pool. On the way out of the driveway with the two children in the car, Dave's foot slipped off the brake at the same time as his hand slid the shift from reverse through neutral into drive. The result was that Dave accelerated his car into the side of his own house. Dave's daughter was not injured, but Jenny Carten, the next door neighbor was injured. In addition, Dave did substantial damage to his home and car.

Dave has been sued by the parents of Jenny Carten and has turned over this claim to New Federal Insurance Co., his automobile liability insurance carrier. In addition, Dave has turned the reports of damage to his house and car over to Federal as Federal insures Dave's house as well as his automobiles.

Questions

1. The Attorney for Jenny Carten's family found out from the attorney hired by New Federal that the adjuster for New Federal was Albert Oakley.

The Attorney called Oakley to discuss possible settlement of the matter, but Oakley indicated: "We don't settle any cases. Thanks for calling--we'll see you in court." Is this proper? Why or why not?

2. Dave Davis, after submitting his claim for damage to his car and house found that the Adjuster handling the case was Albert Oakley. Dave called Oakley to discuss the damage claim and Oakley indicated: "I'm sorry Dave. We don't discuss cases that lead to litigation. You should talk to a lawyer and file suit and we'll see you in court." Is this proper? What facts of Question 2.) change the insurer-insured relationship which exists in Question 1.)? Does that change make a difference?

3. If you found either the actions in Question 1.) or 2). improper, and assuming that there is no statutorily prescribed remedy, how can damages be measured?

Problem 160

Barris Construction Co. had a contract with BCI Enterprises to tear down BCI's existing building at 1117 Linden St. so that the building could be replaced with a new, expanded facility. Arnold Barris, a principle of Barris Construction wrote the address down on the "Specifications" for the job and turned it over to Walter O'Toole, Barris' foreman. O'Toole took the Specifications and he and his crew tore down the building located at 117 Linden, the address which Arnold Barris had mistakenly written down. Sideline Sporting Goods, the owner of 1117 Linden, has now sued Barris Construction for $750,000, the value of the building and the inventory in it at the time of its destruction. Barris Construction has liability insurance with First Flight Insurance Co. which provides Barris with liability of $500,000 for each covered loss. First Flight has provided Barris with a defense to Sideline Sporting Goods' action, and the attorney has deposed Sideline officers and employees and has determined that the inventory alone inside the building was worth over $300,000. In addition, the building had recently been appraised at $300,000.

Questions

1. What obligations does First Flight have to settle the case at this point?

2. At what point, if ever, must First Flight offer the entire $500,000?

3. If First Flight is obligated to offer the entire $500,000 and does not, can First Flight be subject to additional liability?

4. In regards to any liability of First Flight for either failing to pursue settlement or failing to properly settle, discuss the company's liability and their potential damage exposure under the following legal theories:

    a. Breach of the Liability Insurance Contract;

    b. Tort of Negligence Failure to Pursue or Settle;

    c. Absence of Good Faith in Settlement Negotiations;

Notes

E. FISCHER & P. SWISHER, Principles of Insurance Law, *Gruenberg v. Aetna Ins. Co.*, p. 519; notes & questions, p. 523; *Commercial Union Ins. Co. v. Ford Motor Co.*, p. 524; notes & questions, pp. 529-530; *Carter v. Safeco Ins. Co.*, p. 530 (Matthew Bender, 1986); R. HENDERSON, Insurance Law, *Brown v. Guarantee Ins. Co.*, p. 711; notes, p. 717; *Comunale v. Traders & General Ins. Co.*, p. 717; *Crisci v. Security Ins. Co.*, p. 720; *Crisci v. Security Ins. Co.*, p. 720; notes, pp. 725-26 (Michie, 1989); R. JERRY, Understanding Insurance Law, §112 (Matthew Bender, 1987); R. KEETON & A. WIDISS, Insurance Law, 7.8 (West, 1988); R. KEETON, Basic Insurance Law, *Amsden v. Grinnell Mutual Reinsurance Co.*, p. 803;

Gruenberg v. Aetna Ins. Co., p. 807; *United States Fidelity & Guaranty Co. v. Peterson*, p. 811; *Abrams v. Factory Mutual Liability Ins. Co.*, p. 831; *Johansen v. California State Automobile Ass'n Inter-Insurance Bureau*, p. 851; *Rova Farms Resort, Inc. v. Investors Ins. Co.*, p. 860; A Proposal for Legislation, pp. 868-69; *Continental Casualty Co. v. Reserve Ins. Co.*, p. 869 (West, 1977); A. WIDISS, Insurance, Conflicting Interests Under Liability Insurance, p. 739; The Liability Insurer's Duty to Insureds Regarding Settlement, p. 753; *Brakeman v. Potomac Ins. Co.*, p. 754; Mowry v. Badger State Mut. Cas. Co. , p. 757; Note: Strict Liability When an Insurer Rejects a Settlement, p. 772; *Guarantee Abstract & Title Co. v. Interstate Fire & Cas. Co., Inc.*, p. 789; *Aetna Casualty & Surety Co. v. Broadway Arms Corp.*, p. 793; Settlement Negotiations, pp. 772-780; Arbitration, pp. 883-87; Judicial Review, p. 887 (West, 1989); K. YORK & J. WHELAN, Insurance Law (Second Edition), Preliminary Note, pp. 118-19; *Betts v. Allstate Ins. Co.*, p. 119; *Beck v. Farmers Ins. Exchange*, p. 134; notes, pp. 142-45; *Murphy v. Allstate Ins. Co.*, p. 130; *Continental Casualty Co. v. Reserve Ins. Co.*, p. 695 (West, 1988).

2. Statutory Damage/Penalty Provisions

Problem 161

Wanda Flemming was seriously injured when she mistakenly knocked on the door of the Marion Diction Co. and awakened the security guard, who had been sleeping. Instinctively, the guard started shooting at the door and Wanda was hit by bullets in the shoulder and arm. As it turns out, Wanda was looking for another building. As a result of the incident, Wanda sued Marion Diction based upon negligent supervision of the security guard, who was a Marion employee, as well as the direct negligence of the employee alleging that the sign at the front of the building indicated: "Callers should knock to gain entrance," and that Wanda had thought the building was that of a different company. Wanda was confined to a hospital for 3 weeks, lost the use of most of the muscles in the injured shoulder, was required to have several surgical procedures, and lost approximately 6 months work. Marion Diction is insured for $100,000 for liability by Webster Hills Insurance Company. The adjuster for

Marion offered Wanda $1,000 in full settlement of the claim, which was refused and the adjuster would not further discuss the case. At trial, the jury awarded Wanda $750,000 in damages. Marion has now alleged that the settlement practices of Webster Hills was inappropriate. State Statute provides for payment of damages for "Vexatious Refusal:"

> In any action against an insurance company to recover the amount of any loss under a policy of liability, life, health, accident or property insurance, if it appears from the evidence that such company has refused to pay such loss without reasonable cause or excuse, the court or jury may, in addition to the amount of any damages in the case, allow the plaintiff additional damages in an amount not to exceed twenty percent of the first fifteen hundred dollars of the loss, and ten percent of the amount of the loss in excess over fifteen hundred dollars, together with a reasonable attorney's fee.

After post-trial negotiations between Wanda's attorney and the attorney for Webster Hills broke down, Wanda filed suit against Webster Hills, alleging that Webster Hills breached its insurance contract with Marion, negligently failed to negotiate a settlement with Wanda, and breached the statutory provision.

Questions

1. As to the various claims:

    a. How does Wanda have a contract claim against Webster Hills?

    b. What tort duty is owed to Wanda by Webster Hills?

    c. Was the purpose of the statute to protect injured third parties or those in a contract relationship with an insurance company? How, then, can Wanda maintain the claim?

2. Webster Hills moves to dismiss the contract and tort claims. What result? Why?

3. Assume that the statute, instead of the provision in the problem, provided:

> It is hereby declared to be an Unfair Insurance Settlement Practice for any insurance company to fail to attempt, in good faith, to effectuate prompt, fair and equitable settlement of claims submitted in which liability of the company has become reasonably clear.

When Webster Hills Insurance refused to further bargain, the company was sued by Wanda based upon the statute. Webster Hills moved to dismiss claiming that the statute did not create a private cause of action. What result? Why?

Notes

R. HENDERSON, Insurance Law, *Tank v. State Farm Fire & Cas. Co.*, p. 765; notes, pp. 768-770 (Michie, 1989); R. JERRY, Understanding Insurance Law, §22[d] (Matthew Bender, 1987); R. KEETON & A. WIDISS, Insurance Law, §7.7 (West, 1988); R. KEETON, Basic Insurance Law, *Seguin v. Continental Service Life & Health Ins. Co.*, p. 795 (West, 1977); A. WIDISS, Insurance, Statutory Remedies for Nonpayment or Late Payment of Insurance Claims, p. 742; 751; *D'Ambrosio v. Pennsylvania National Mut. Cas. Co.*, p. 743 (West, 1989); K. YORK & J. WHELAN, Insurance Law (Second Edition), Note, pp. 145-47; *Royal Globe Ins. Co. v. Superior Court of Butte County*, p. 147;[2] notes, 157-59 (West, 1988).

3. *Settlement of Malpractice Cases*

PROBLEM 162

[2]. As suggested in the prefatory note to *Royal Globe*, the decision was indeed overruled in *Moradi-Shalal v. Fireman's Fund Ins. Co.*, 46 Cal.3d 287, 250 Cal.Rptr. 116, 758 P.2d 58 (1988).

Alice West, M.D. misread an X-Ray of her patient, Herbert Scooner. As a result, Scooner suffered extensive damage to the leg for which he sued West for malpractice. West has a malpractice insurance policy with Perfect Casualty Co. The policy provides for settlement of any claim against the insured as follows:

> The insurer is empowered to make such investigation and negotiation and, with the written consent of the insured, such settlement of any claim or suit as the company deems expedient.

While negotiating with the attorneys for Mr. Scooner, Perfect's Insurance Adjuster asked Alice to sign the following release:

> The Insured herein authorizes the Insurer (Perfect Casualty Co.) to settle the claim of Herbert Scooner against the insured within the limits of my policy with Perfect Casualty Co.

Alice agreed to these provisions and signed the letter. Thereafter, the Adjuster settled the claim for $250,000 which was within the terms of the policy. Alice is now angry that she was not consulted before a settlement was finalized and has sued Perfect Casualty Co. based upon its unfair settlement practices. Does Alice have a claim? If she does, what is her damage? Why would the insured want the "written consent" provision in this type of insurance?

E. Special Legal Ethics Issues in Insurance Litigation

Problem 163

Dr. Richard Mann, M.D. was the physician in charge of Memorial

Hospital one evening when a call came in about a serious automobile accident. Police on the scene indicated that one of the persons injured would not appear to be able to survive transport to the hospital. As a result, Dr. Mann left another doctor in charge of the Emergency Room and rode with the ambulance to the scene. At the scene, Dr. Mann gave emergency care to Randa Williams, the injured person about whom the police had been concerned. By the time another ambulance had taken other injured persons to the hospital, Dr. Mann believed that Williams could be transported to the hospital. As Dr. Mann and the ambulance driver attempted to lift the stretcher holding Wanda into the ambulance, the driver severely strained his back and could not straighten without severe pain. Dr. Mann had the driver lie down in the back of the ambulance and Dr. Mann drove. He turned on both the ambulance's sirens and lights, and proceeded at breakneck speed for Memorial Hospital. At the first traffic light, which was red against him, Dr. Mann did not slow down until he struck another car, proceeding through a green light. The driver of the car struck by Dr. Mann, Robert Sanford, had heard the sirens and was trying to figure out where they were coming from when the collision took place. State law provides that an ambulance can proceed through a red light only in the event of a life threatening emergency and then only if the ambulance slows to assure that the intersection is clear. State law has also been interpreted to require all drivers to slow and pull to the side of the road when the driver hears fire, police or ambulance sirens. As a result of the accident, Randa Williams died and Robert Sanford was injured. Memorial Hospital and Dr. Mann each have Professional Liability (Malpractice) Insurance with Reliable Insurance Co. Both Memorial Hospital and Robert Sanford have automobile liability insurance with Autotrust Insurance Co.

Questions

1. The family of Randa Williams filed a malpractice action against Dr. Mann alleging that, once her condition had stabilized, there was no emergency and that she did not need to be rushed to Memorial Hospital. Thus, they claimed that Dr. Mann's speeding was negligent medical treatment of Randa, a claim which the doctor sent on to Reliable. Dr. Mann's malpractice policy limited coverage to "medical incidents," and defined this term as "any act or omission in the furnishing of professional medical services by the insured." Because initial investigation of the case indicated that Dr. Mann could have been driving so fast because he believed that Randa needed to be transported quickly, Reliable agreed to defend and hired Samantha Simon, Esq., to defend the case. What ethical problems arise for Simon at this stage?

2. Assume that Reliable had been willing to take the case only with a Reservation of Rights letter indicating their belief that driving the ambulance was not a "medical incident" within the meaning of the policy.

   a. If that letter is received by Dr. Mann after Samantha Smith has been hired, what are the obligations of Smith?

   b. If that letter is received by Dr. Mann before Samantha Smith has been hired, what are the obligations of Smith?

   c. What are Smith's options, under either a.) or b.) above, if Dr. Mann seeks Smith's help in interpreting this letter?

3. Assume that Reliable had been willing to take the case only with a "Nonwaiver Agreement" preserving the right of Reliable to contest that driving

the ambulance was not a "medical incident" within the meaning of the policy. What are Smith's obligations when Dr. Mann seeks Smith's help in interpreting this agreement?

4. In her first meeting with Dr. Mann, Samantha inquired as to how the accident happened. Dr. Mann stated: "Oh, I knew that the patient was stable, but I had never driven an ambulance before and just wanted to see how fast it could go." What ethical problems arise for Samantha?

5. Assume that the Williams' attorney indicated to Samantha that the Williams family was willing to take $25,000 in settlement of the claim and that Samantha has the approval of Reliable to accept this amount. Dr. Mann steadfastly refuses to allow Samantha to accept the offer. What can Samantha do?

6. Assume that Samantha concluded that the liability of Dr. Mann was substantial and that it was highly likely that Reliable would be required to pay. When the attorney for Williams indicates a willingness by the clients to accept a $25,000 settlement, and Dr. Mann agrees with that amount, Reliable balks, and says: "Offer them $500." That offer is immediately refused. The case proceeds to trial and results in a judgment against Dr. Mann $50,000 in excess of all applicable insurance. Can Dr. Mann successfully assert a claim against Samantha?

Notes

R. HENDERSON, Insurance Law, *Rawlings v. Apodaca*, p. 5 (Michie, 1989); R. JERRY, Understanding Insurance Law, §114 (Matthew Bender, 1987); R. KEETON & A. WIDISS, Insurance Law, §§7.6(b), (c) (West, 1988); R. KEETON, Basic Insurance Law, *Pennix v. Winton*, p. 836; *O'Morrow v. Borad*, p. 836; *Perkoski v. Wilson*, p. 837; *Jedwabny v. Philadelphia Transportation Co.*, p. 848; *Henke v. Iowa Home Mutual Casualty Co.*, p. 873; *Murach v. Massachusetts Bonding & Ins. Co.*, p. 875; *Goad v. Fisher*, p.

877; *Ross v. Stricker*, p. 884 (West, 1977); A. WIDISS, Insurance, *San Diego Navy Federal Credit Union v. Cumis Ins. Society, Inc.*, p. 826 (West, 1989); K. YORK & J. WHELAN, Insurance Law (Second Edition), note, pp. 127-130 (West, 1988); W. YOUNG & E. HOLMES, Insurance, *Richmond v. Georgia Farm Mut. Ins. Co.*, p. 309; *Employers Casualty Co. v. Tilley*, p. 315; Duties of Insurers and Attorneys Employed to Represent Insureds, p. 317; Effect of Non-Waiver Agreement, p. 319; Effect of Subsequent Conduct of Employers and Attorney, p. 320; notes, p. 321; "Guiding Principle VI," p. 321; *Parsons v. Continental Nat. American Group*, p. 322; notes, p. 325 (Foundation, 1985).

See also American Bar Association, Model Code of Professional Responsibility, D.R. 5-105; American Bar Association, Model Rules of Professional Conduct, Rules 1.7, 1.8; C. WOLFRAM, Modern Legal Ethics, 8.4 (West, 1986).